Decimals

> Turn to each section to find a more detailed skills list.

Table of Contents

What Does This Book Include?

- More than 80 student practice pages that reinforce adding, subtracting, multiplying, and dividing decimals
- A detailed skills list for each section of the book
- Send-home letters informing parents of the skills being targeted and ways to practice these skills
- Student checkups
- A reproducible student progress chart
- Awards to celebrate student progress
- Answer keys for easy checking
- Perforated pages for easy removal and filing if desired

What Are the Benefits of This Book?

- Organized for quick and easy use
- Enhances and supports your existing math program
- Offers multiple practice opportunities
- Helps develop mastery of basic facts
- Provides reinforcement for different ability levels
- Includes communications pages that encourage parents' participation in their children's learning of math
- Contains checkups that assess students' decimal knowledge
- Offers a reproducible chart for documenting student progress
- Aligns with national math standards

©2004 by THE EDUCATION CENTER, INC.
All rights reserved.
ISBN# 1-56234-589-3

How to Use This Book
Steps to Success

Choose Skills to Target

Scan the detailed table of contents at the beginning of each section to find just the right skills to target your students' needs.

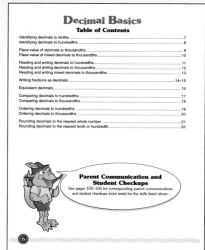

Select Fun Practice Pages

Choose from a variety of fun formats the pages that best match your students' current ability levels.

Fun Formats

Date Skill Completed

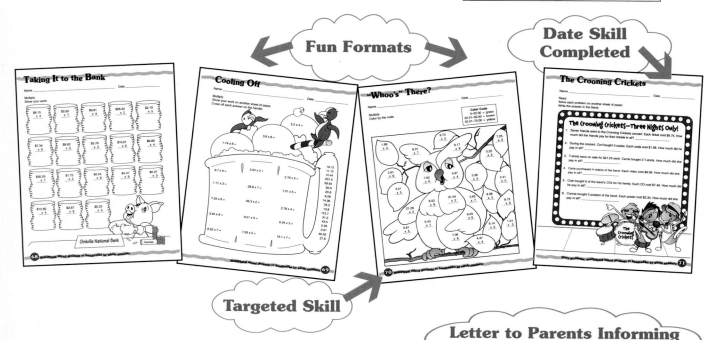

Targeted Skill

Letter to Parents Informing Them of Skill to Review

Communicate With Parents

Recruit parent assistance by locating the appropriate parent letter (pages 102–130), making copies, and sending the letter home.

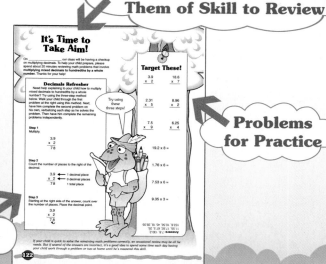

Decimal Review for Parents

Problems for Practice

Assess Student Understanding

Assess students' progress with student checkups (mini tests) on pages 103–131. Choose Checkup A or Checkup B.

Checkup 11

Name _____ Date _____

Multiply.

A. 2.5   3.5   4.83   5.06
   x 8   x 9   x 4   x 3

B. 11.8   2.39   9.2   16.4
   x 7   x 6   x 5   x 2

C. 7.4 x 3 =   19.36 x 5 =

D. 6.4 x 8 =   9.06 x 4 =

Test A: Multiplying mixed decimals to hundredths by whole numbers

Checkup 11

Name _____ Date _____

Multiply.

A. 12.8   3.64   2.4   8.6
   x 9   x 7   x 5   x 4

B. 9.72   7.41   5.3   11.9
   x 3   x 2   x 8   x 6

C. 13.6 x 4 =   7.63 x 3 =

D. 5.42 x 6 =   9.4 x 9 =

Test B: Multiplying mixed decimals to hundredths by whole numbers

Two Checkups for Each Skill

Document Progress

Documenting student progress can be as easy as 1, 2, 3! Do the following for each student:

1. Make a copy of the Student Progress Charts (pages 100–101).
2. File the chart in his math portfolio or a class notebook.
3. Record the date each checkup is given, the number of correct answers, and any comments regarding his progress.

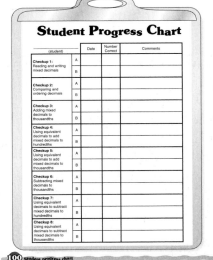

Student Progress Chart

(student)		Date	Number Correct	Comments
Checkup 1: Reading and writing mixed decimals	A			
	B			
Checkup 2: Comparing and ordering decimals	A			
	B			
Checkup 3: Adding mixed decimals to thousandths	A			
	B			
Checkup 4: Using equivalent decimals to add mixed decimals to hundredths	A			
	B			
Checkup 5: Using equivalent decimals to add mixed decimals to thousandths	A			
	B			
Checkup 6: Subtracting mixed decimals to thousandths	A			
	B			
Checkup 7: Using equivalent decimals to subtract mixed decimals to hundredths	A			
	B			
Checkup 8: Using equivalent decimals to subtract mixed decimals to thousandths	A			
	B			

100 Student progress chart

Celebrate!

Celebrate decimal success using the awards on page 132.

You're on the Mark!

_____
student

mastered multiplying decimals.

_____
date

Books in the Target Math Success series include

- *Basic Addition Facts to 18*
- *Basic Subtraction Facts to 18*
- *Addition of Larger Numbers*
- *Subtraction of Larger Numbers*
- *Basic Multiplication Facts and More*
- *Basic Division Facts and More*
- *Multiplication of Larger Numbers*
- *Division of Larger Numbers*
- *Fractions*
- *Decimals*

Also Available From Your Friends at *The Mailbox*®:

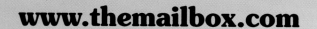

Decimal Basics

Decimal Basics
Table of Contents

Parent Communication and Student Checkups

See pages 102–105 for corresponding parent communications and student checkups (mini tests) on reading and writing mixed decimals and comparing and ordering decimals.

Picnic Lunch

Name _____ Date _____

Write the decimal for the shaded part of each model.
The first one has been done for you.

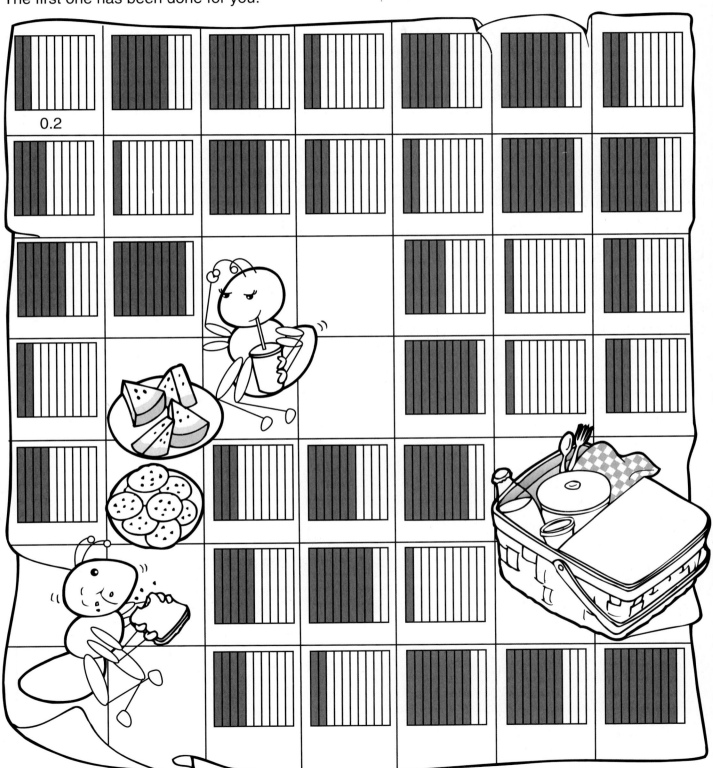

0.2

Slam Dunk!

Name _____   Date _____

Write the decimal for the shaded part of each model.
Cross out the matching answer on the pole.

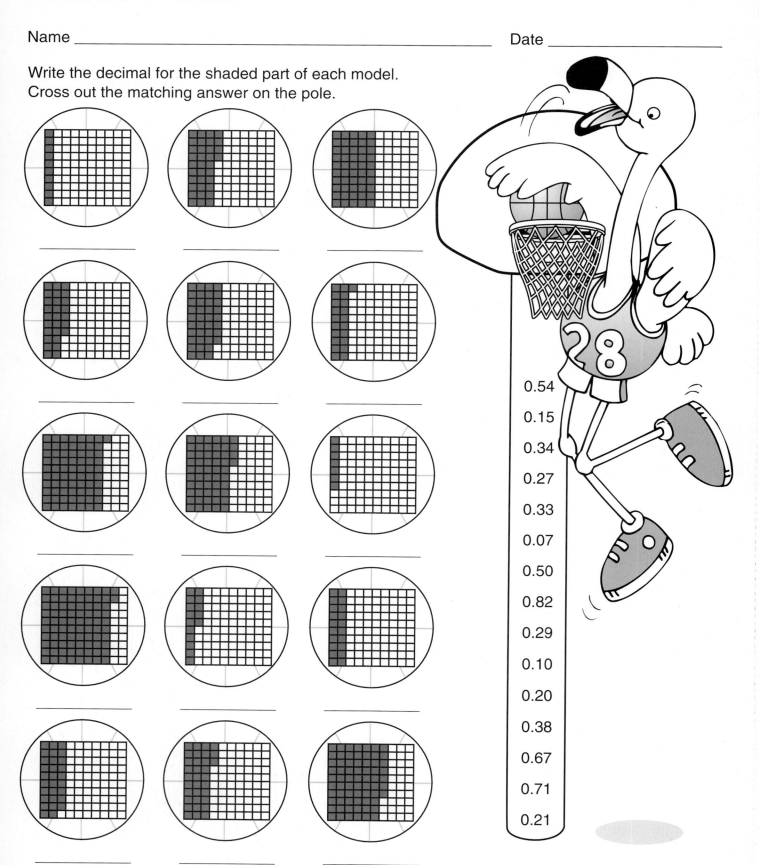

0.54
0.15
0.34
0.27
0.33
0.07
0.50
0.82
0.29
0.10
0.20
0.38
0.67
0.71
0.21

Identifying decimals to hundredths

Magic Show

Name _____ Date _____

Circle the digit in the place noted in parentheses.
Write the circled digit in the magic square below.
The sum of each row and column should equal 20.

① 0.14
(tenths)

② 0.789
(thousandths)

③ 0.36
(hundredths)

④ 0.054
(thousandths)

⑤ 0.981
(tenths)

⑥ 0.315
(hundredths)

⑦ 0.76
(tenths)

⑧ 0.043
(thousandths)

⑨ 0.247
(hundredths)

⑩ 0.651
(thousandths)

⑪ 0.57
(hundredths)

⑫ 0.805
(tenths)

⑬ 0.016
(thousandths)

⑭ 0.92
(tenths)

⑮ 0.007
(hundredths)

⑯ 0.593
(tenths)

I don't like this! Can't we just do the hat trick again?

And now for my saw-the-rabbit-in-half trick!

1	2	3	4
5	6	7	8
9	10	11	12
13	14	15	16

Star Light, Star Bright

Name ______________________________ Date ________________

Identify the place of the underlined digit.
Color by the code.

Code
ones or tens = blue
tenths = yellow
hundredths = red
thousandths = green

5.431
25.755
78.03
10.247
9.042
8.56
12.077
6.124
15.009
3.045
37.92
42.257
17.568
48.05
20.837
18.07
6.09
14.55
77.452
99.006
84.313
53.679
12.5
4.71
17.9
3.453
60.35
61.094
8.05
34.007
80.702
45.678

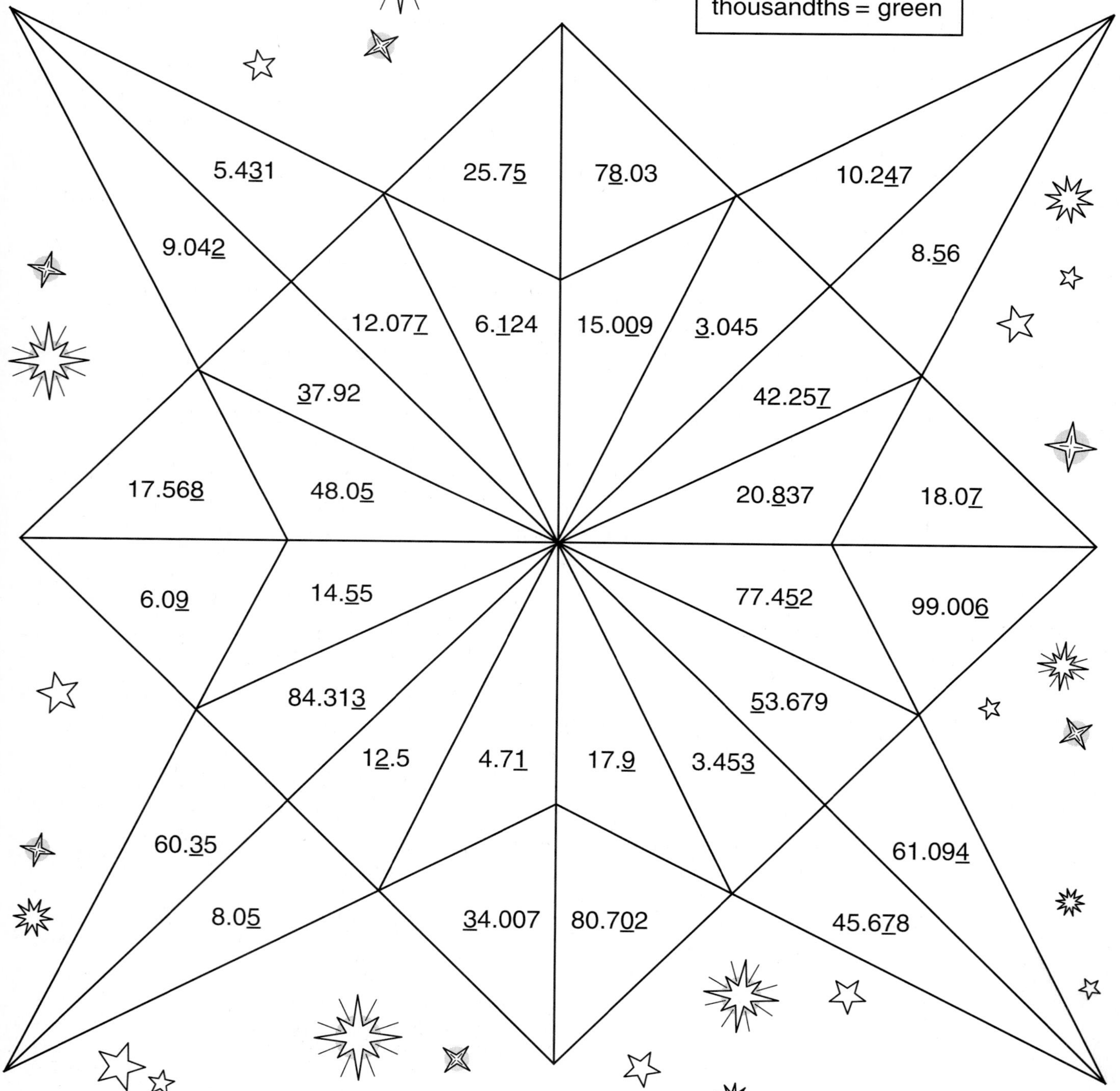

And the Winner Is...

Name ______________________________ Date ______________

Read the standard form of the decimal. Color the correct expanded or written form to show the path to the winner.

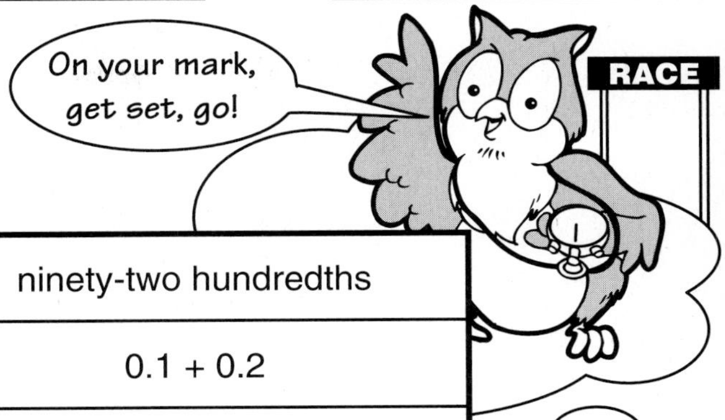
On your mark, get set, go!
RACE

0.92	0.9 + 0.2	ninety-two hundredths
0.12	twelve hundredths	0.1 + 0.2
0.35	thirty-five hundreds	0.3 + 0.05
0.46	0.4 + 0.06	four tenths
0.5	five tenths	five hundredths
0.72	seventy-two hundreds	seventy-two hundredths
0.67	sixty-seven	0.6 + 0.07
0.28	0.2 + 0.08	twenty-eight tenths
0.19	0.01 + 0.9	nineteen hundredths
0.22	two tenths	0.2 + 0.02
0.7	seven hundredths	seven tenths
0.86	eighty-six hundredths	0.08 + 0.06
0.24	twenty-four tenths	0.2 + 0.04
0.53	0.5 + 0.03	fifty-three hundreds
	hummingbird	**hawk**

311
231

Kite Release

Name _____   Date _____

Read each decimal in written and standard form.
Find each matching kite and T-shirt. Color each pair a different color.

eleven
thousandths

fifteen
hundredths

five
thousandths

one
tenth

fifty-three
thousandths

sixty-two
hundredths

eight
tenths

four
thousandths

twenty-two
hundredths

three hundred
twenty-one
thousandths

seven
tenths

0.1

0.053

0.004

0.15

0.321

0.62

0.22

0.011

0.7

0.005

0.8

Reading and writing decimals to thousandths

Got Jelly?

Name _____ Date _____

Read the written form of each decimal.
Write the decimal in standard form.
Cross off the answer on the coral.

two and
eight tenths

_____

seventy-eight
and two
hundredths

_____

eighty-four
and four
hundredths

_____

ten and
thirteen
thousandths

_____

five and
three
thousandths

_____

seventy-eight
and two
tenths

_____

one and
twelve
thousandths

_____

one hundred
twenty-five and
one tenth

_____

forty-five
and sixteen
hundredths

_____

fifteen and
sixty-seven
hundredths

_____

thirty-three
and eight
hundredths

_____

six and three
hundred
twenty-five
thousandths

_____

6.325   78.2   33.08

10.013   78.02   1.012

125.1   5.003   84.04   45.16

2.8   15.67   96.5

No Place Like Home!

Name _____   Date _____

Color if correct.
Connect the colored boxes to draw a path to the magic lamp.

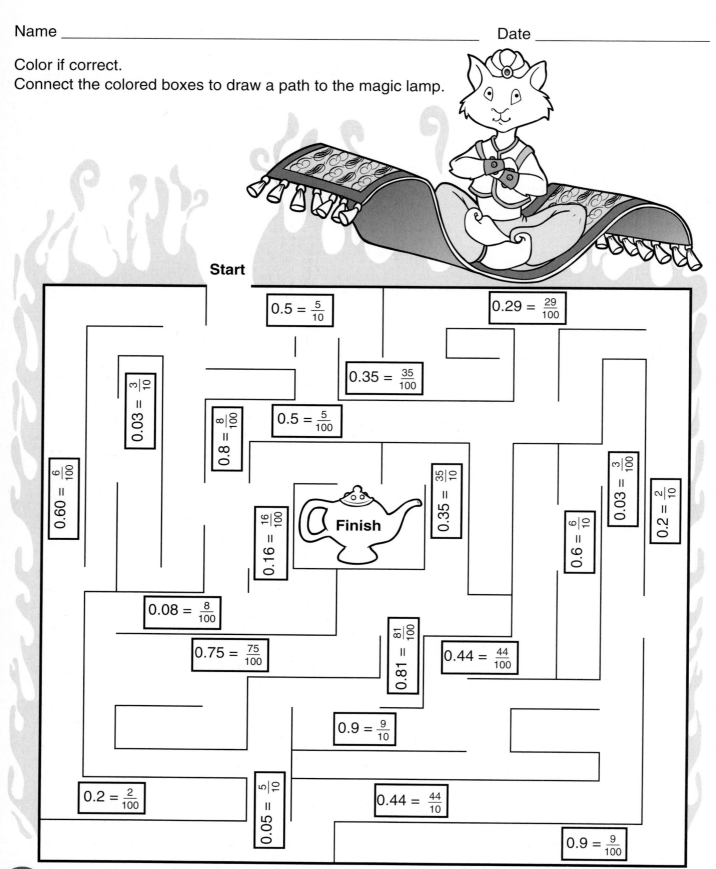

Start

$0.5 = \frac{5}{10}$

$0.29 = \frac{29}{100}$

$0.35 = \frac{35}{100}$

$0.03 = \frac{3}{10}$

$0.8 = \frac{8}{100}$

$0.5 = \frac{5}{100}$

$0.60 = \frac{6}{100}$

$0.16 = \frac{16}{100}$

Finish

$0.35 = \frac{35}{10}$

$0.03 = \frac{3}{100}$

$0.2 = \frac{2}{10}$

$0.6 = \frac{6}{10}$

$0.08 = \frac{8}{100}$

$0.75 = \frac{75}{100}$

$0.81 = \frac{81}{100}$

$0.44 = \frac{44}{100}$

$0.9 = \frac{9}{10}$

$0.2 = \frac{2}{100}$

$0.05 = \frac{5}{10}$

$0.44 = \frac{44}{10}$

$0.9 = \frac{9}{100}$

Hmmm?

Name _____ Date _____

Write the equivalent decimal on the line.

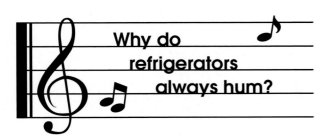

Why do refrigerators always hum?

$\frac{59}{100}$ = _____ Ⓣ

$\frac{25}{100}$ = _____ Ⓗ

$\frac{3}{10}$ = _____ Ⓨ

$\frac{7}{100}$ = _____ Ⓝ

$\frac{52}{100}$ = _____ Ⓞ

$\frac{9}{10}$ = _____ Ⓗ

$\frac{46}{100}$ = _____ Ⓞ

$\frac{15}{100}$ = _____ Ⓒ

$\frac{20}{100}$ = _____ Ⓔ

$\frac{83}{100}$ = _____ Ⓦ

$\frac{4}{10}$ = _____ Ⓣ

$\frac{8}{10}$ = _____ Ⓞ

$\frac{18}{100}$ = _____ Ⓝ

$\frac{5}{100}$ = _____ Ⓚ

$\frac{98}{100}$ = _____ Ⓔ

$\frac{60}{100}$ = _____ Ⓓ

$\frac{5}{10}$ = _____ Ⓡ

$\frac{75}{100}$ = _____ ❗

$\frac{10}{100}$ = _____ Ⓣ

$\frac{12}{100}$ = _____ Ⓓ

$\frac{42}{100}$ = _____ Ⓢ

$\frac{63}{100}$ = _____ Ⓦ

To solve the riddle, write the circled letter in the matching blank.

Because   ___ ___ ___ ___   ___ ___ ___ ___ ___
         0.59 0.9 0.98 0.3   0.60 0.52 0.07 0.15 0.4

___ ___ ___ ___   ___ ___ ___   ___ ___ ___ ___ ___ ___
0.05 0.18 0.46 0.83   0.10 0.25 0.20   0.63 0.8 0.5 0.12 0.42 0.75

Gotta Be Picky!

Name _____ Date _____

Color the eggs in each nest that have equivalent decimals.

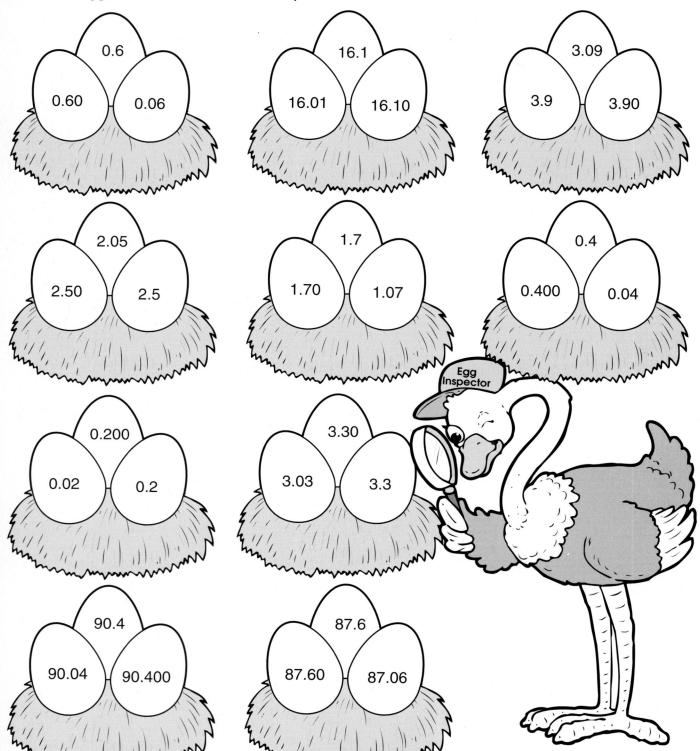

0.6 0.60 0.06

16.1 16.01 16.10

3.09 3.9 3.90

2.05 2.50 2.5

1.7 1.70 1.07

0.4 0.400 0.04

0.200 0.02 0.2

3.30 3.03 3.3

Egg Inspector

90.4 90.04 90.400

87.6 87.60 87.06

Equivalent decimals

Underwater Surprise

Name _____   Date _____

Compare the decimals.
Write <, >, or = in each blank.
Color by the code.

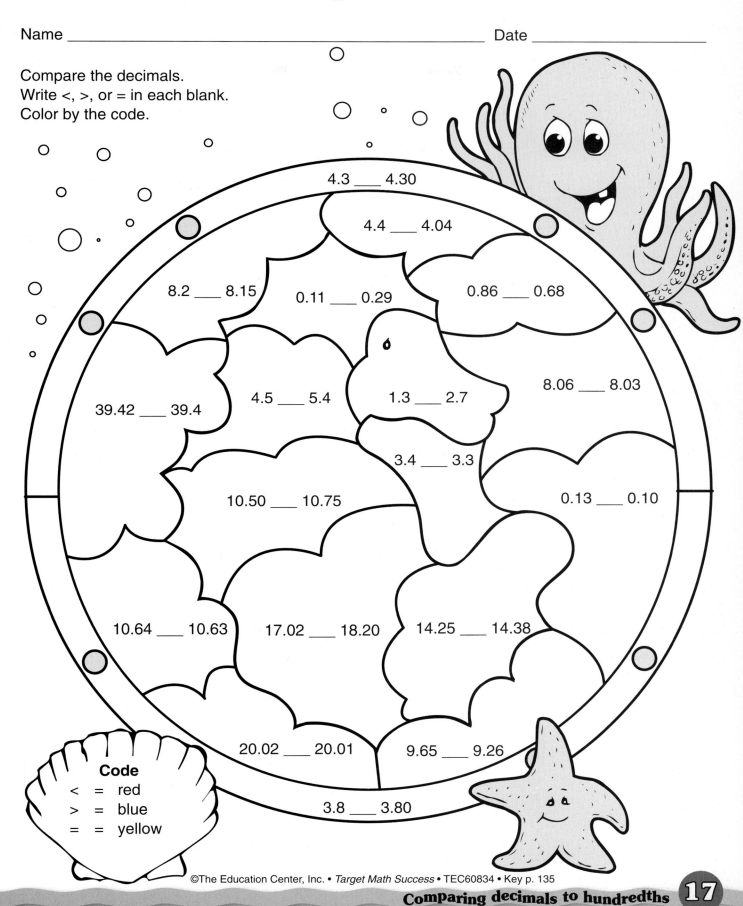

4.3 ___ 4.30

4.4 ___ 4.04

8.2 ___ 8.15   0.11 ___ 0.29   0.86 ___ 0.68

8.06 ___ 8.03

39.42 ___ 39.4   4.5 ___ 5.4   1.3 ___ 2.7

3.4 ___ 3.3

0.13 ___ 0.10

10.50 ___ 10.75

10.64 ___ 10.63   17.02 ___ 18.20   14.25 ___ 14.38

20.02 ___ 20.01   9.65 ___ 9.26

3.8 ___ 3.80

Code
< = red
> = blue
= = yellow

What's Ashore?

Compare the decimals.
Color blue if correct.
To solve the riddle, write the colored letters in order
in the blanks below.

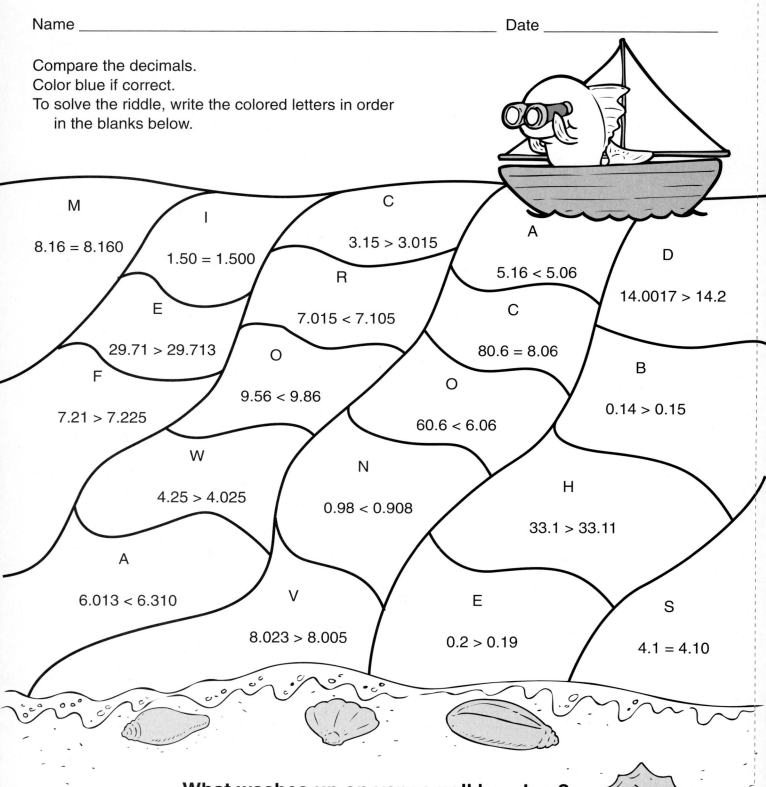

M
8.16 = 8.160

I
1.50 = 1.500

C
3.15 > 3.015

A
5.16 < 5.06

D
14.0017 > 14.2

E
29.71 > 29.713

R
7.015 < 7.105

C
80.6 = 8.06

F
7.21 > 7.225

O
9.56 < 9.86

O
60.6 < 6.06

B
0.14 > 0.15

W
4.25 > 4.025

N
0.98 < 0.908

H
33.1 > 33.11

A
6.013 < 6.310

V
8.023 > 8.005

E
0.2 > 0.19

S
4.1 = 4.10

What washes up on very small beaches?

___ ___ ___ ___ ___ ___ ___ ___

Comparing decimals to thousandths

Love at First Sight!

Name _____ Date _____

If the decimals are correctly ordered from least to greatest,
color the milk or cookie.

2.31	45.07
6.5	45.57
9.86	45.7

5.2	23.0
5.17	57.8
4.95	41.03

0.82	1.7
0.81	1.3
0.80	1.0

7.68	13.94
7.8	13.95
8.06	14.94
8.7	

17.09	0.08
17.90	0.9
17.89	8.0

0.21	6.53
0.27	6.5
0.22	6.35
	6.30

5.40	2.01
5.41	2.05
5.39	2.07

18.99	61.73
19.10	64.82
19.19	64.87
	64.99

Who's the Skateboard Superstar?

Name _____ Date _____

Order the decimals from least to greatest.
Color the matching boxes to show the path
to the skateboard superstar.

7.60, 7.650, 7.560 =	7.60, 7.650, 7.560	7.650, 7.60, 7.560	7.560, 7.60, 7.650
8.064, 9.06, 9.46 =	9.46, 9.06, 8.064	8.064, 9.06, 9.46	9.06, 9.46, 8.064
23.7, 23.07, 23.702 =	23.702, 23.7, 23.07	23.07, 23.7, 23.702	23.7, 23.702, 23.07
56.3, 56.93, 56.039 =	56.039, 56.3, 56.93	56.93, 56.3, 56.039	56.3, 56.93, 56.039
4.57, 4.057, 45.7 =	4.057, 4.57, 45.7	4.57, 45.7, 4.057	45.7, 4.57, 4.057
4.687, 4.874, 4.784 =	4.687, 4.784, 4.874	4.784, 4.687, 4.874	4.874, 4.784, 4.687
8.023, 8.09, 8.057 =	8.023, 8.057, 8.09	8.09, 8.057, 8.023	8.057, 8.09, 8.023
15.820, 15.280, 15.0 =	15.280, 15.0, 15.820	15.0, 15.280, 15.820	15.820, 15.280, 15.0
40.628, 34.628, 43.628 =	34.628, 40.628, 43.628	43.628, 40.628, 34.628	40.628, 34.628, 43.628
62.601, 6.26, 62.610 =	62.610, 62.601, 6.26	6.26, 62.601, 62.610	62.601, 6.26, 62.610

High Flyer   **Speedy Roller**   **Super Twister**

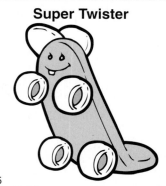

Adding Decimals
Table of Contents

Parent Communication and Student Checkups

*See pages 106–111 for corresponding parent communications and student checkups (mini tests) for these skills.

Monkey Business

Name _____ Date _____

Add.

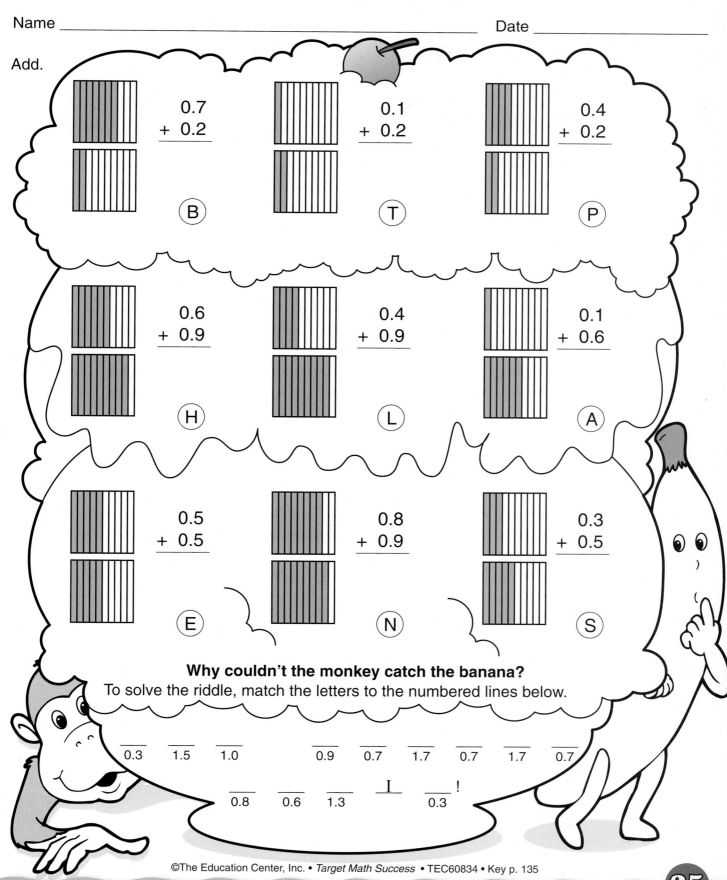

$$0.7 + 0.2$$ Ⓑ

$$0.1 + 0.2$$ Ⓣ

$$0.4 + 0.2$$ Ⓟ

$$0.6 + 0.9$$ Ⓗ

$$0.4 + 0.9$$ Ⓛ

$$0.1 + 0.6$$ Ⓐ

$$0.5 + 0.5$$ Ⓔ

$$0.8 + 0.9$$ Ⓝ

$$0.3 + 0.5$$ Ⓢ

Why couldn't the monkey catch the banana?
To solve the riddle, match the letters to the numbered lines below.

――― ――― ―――   ――― ――― ――― ――― ――― ―――
0.3   1.5   1.0   0.9   0.7   1.7   0.7   1.7   0.7

――― ――― ―――   I ―――!
0.8   0.6   1.3   0.3

Cody the Cowboy Cat

Name _____ Date _____

Add.
Cross out the matching answer on the lasso.

Lasso numbers (clockwise): 10.3, 18.1, 12.3, 9.9, 9.0, 4.5, 41.7, 7.1, 2.9, 14.3, 4.7, 14.9, 6.8, 4.2, 10.0, 4.8, 7.6, 12.8, 31.2, 10.5, 8.8, 7.7

$$\begin{array}{r} 5.7 \\ +\ 1.1 \\ \hline \end{array} \qquad \begin{array}{r} 4.7 \\ +\ 2.4 \\ \hline \end{array} \qquad \begin{array}{r} 8.0 \\ +\ 4.3 \\ \hline \end{array} \qquad \begin{array}{r} 2.6 \\ +\ 2.2 \\ \hline \end{array}$$

$$\begin{array}{r} 3.5 \\ +\ 1.2 \\ \hline \end{array} \qquad \begin{array}{r} 0.1 \\ +\ 2.8 \\ \hline \end{array} \qquad \begin{array}{r} 8.3 \\ +\ 0.5 \\ \hline \end{array} \qquad \begin{array}{r} 4.3 \\ +\ 6.2 \\ \hline \end{array}$$

$$\begin{array}{r} 3.3 \\ +\ 1.2 \\ \hline \end{array} \qquad \begin{array}{r} 8.2 \\ +\ 6.1 \\ \hline \end{array} \qquad \begin{array}{r} 0.7 \\ +\ 3.5 \\ \hline \end{array} \qquad \begin{array}{r} 4.4 \\ +\ 3.2 \\ \hline \end{array}$$

$$\begin{array}{r} 7.5 \\ +\ 2.4 \\ \hline \end{array} \qquad \begin{array}{r} 7.8 \\ +\ 2.5 \\ \hline \end{array} \qquad \begin{array}{r} 10.9 \\ +\ 4.0 \\ \hline \end{array} \qquad \begin{array}{r} 22.6 \\ +\ 8.6 \\ \hline \end{array}$$

$$\begin{array}{r} 11.5 \\ +\ 1.3 \\ \hline \end{array} \qquad \begin{array}{r} 4.9 \\ +\ 5.1 \\ \hline \end{array} \qquad \begin{array}{r} 15.9 \\ +\ 2.2 \\ \hline \end{array}$$

$$\begin{array}{r} 40.4 \\ +\ 1.3 \\ \hline \end{array} \qquad \begin{array}{r} 2.6 \\ +\ 5.1 \\ \hline \end{array} \qquad \begin{array}{r} 7.6 \\ +\ 1.4 \\ \hline \end{array}$$

Adding mixed decimals to tenths

Sweet Success!

Name _____ Date _____

Add.
Show your work on another sheet of paper.
Color each pair of matching jelly beans a different color.

14.5 + 25.6 =
_____

85.1 + 26.5 =
_____

23.3 + 32.2 =
_____

16.4 + 32.6 =
_____

7.5 + 19.4 =
_____

45.3 + 10.2 =
_____

12.3 + 54.1 =
_____

82.3 + 101.4 =
_____

312.2 + 658.2 =
_____

63.5 + 2.9 =
_____

97.1 + 14.5 =
_____

825.2 + 145.2 =
_____

17.3 + 22.8 =
_____

254.3 + 345.2 =
_____

2.6 + 24.3 =
_____

118.1 + 65.6 =
_____

6.2 + 42.8 =
_____

444.7 + 154.8 =
_____

98.4 + 245.7 =
_____

313.2 + 30.9 =
_____

3, 2, 1—Zzzz!

Name _____   Date _____

Add.

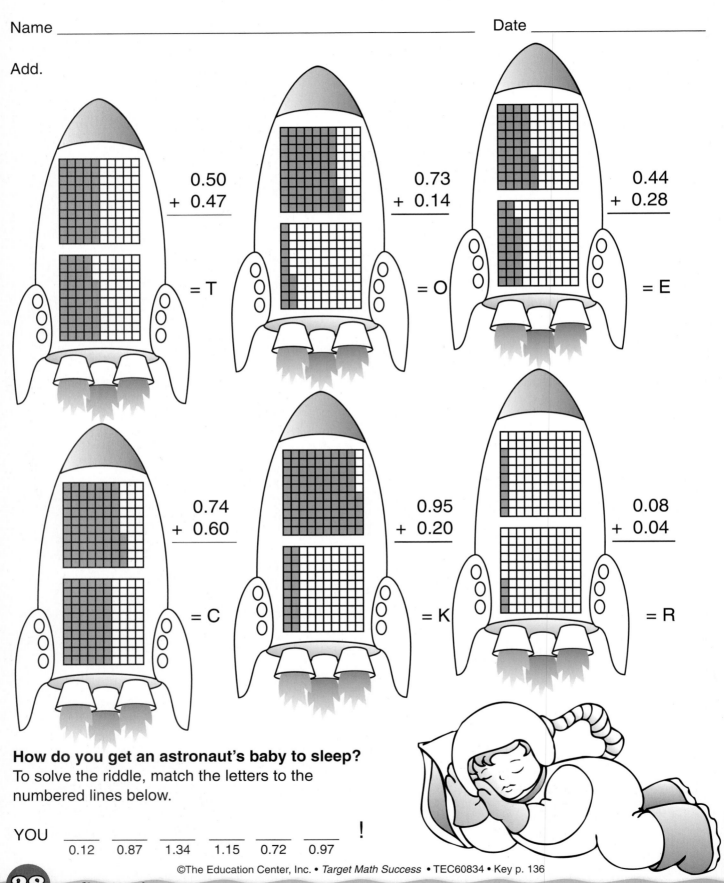

$$\begin{array}{r} 0.50 \\ + 0.47 \\ \hline \end{array}$$ = T

$$\begin{array}{r} 0.73 \\ + 0.14 \\ \hline \end{array}$$ = O

$$\begin{array}{r} 0.44 \\ + 0.28 \\ \hline \end{array}$$ = E

$$\begin{array}{r} 0.74 \\ + 0.60 \\ \hline \end{array}$$ = C

$$\begin{array}{r} 0.95 \\ + 0.20 \\ \hline \end{array}$$ = K

$$\begin{array}{r} 0.08 \\ + 0.04 \\ \hline \end{array}$$ = R

How do you get an astronaut's baby to sleep?
To solve the riddle, match the letters to the numbered lines below.

YOU _____ _____ _____ _____ _____ _____ !
     0.12 0.87 1.34 1.15 0.72 0.97

Crazy-Colored Cow

Name _____   Date _____

Add.
Color by the code.

$$15.16 + 15.39$$

$$55.84 + 6.27$$

$$7.32 + 5.08$$

$$37.66 + 4.08$$

$$78.83 + 65.96$$

$$35.99 + 26.41$$

$$20.29 + 4.18$$

$$73.73 + 9.54$$

$$14.64 + 11.34$$

$$85.95 + 28.63$$

$$44.59 + 5.33$$

$$95.77 + 42.89$$

$$9.17 + 7.33$$

$$30.58 + 15.22$$

$$71.72 + 17.64$$

$$16.09 + 4.06$$

$$30.62 + 29.49$$

$$28.39 + 14.29$$

$$22.31 + 1.02$$

$$48.85 + 8.23$$

Code
0–25 = red
25.01–50 = blue
50.01–100 = green
100–150 = yellow

Adding mixed decimals to hundredths   29

Unidentified Vacation Land

Name _____   Date _____

Add.
Show your work on another sheet of paper.
Color by the code.

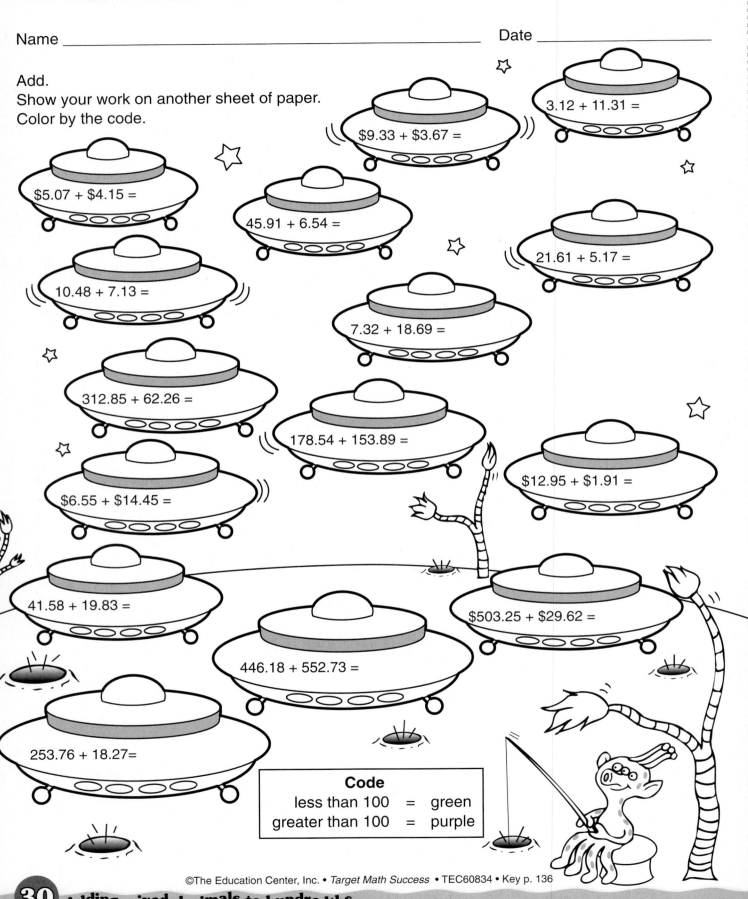

$9.33 + $3.67 =

3.12 + 11.31 =

$5.07 + $4.15 =

45.91 + 6.54 =

21.61 + 5.17 =

10.48 + 7.13 =

7.32 + 18.69 =

312.85 + 62.26 =

178.54 + 153.89 =

$12.95 + $1.91 =

$6.55 + $14.45 =

41.58 + 19.83 =

$503.25 + $29.62 =

446.18 + 552.73 =

253.76 + 18.27=

Code
less than 100   =   green
greater than 100   =   purple

Adding mixed decimals to hundredths

Dr. Callie Coe, Veterinarian

Name _____   Date _____

Add.

What did the veterinarian keep outside her door?

3.215 + 2.147 = E	13.059 + 7.338 = T
53.864 + 44.265 = M	75.926 + 19.157 = L
126.391 + 66.023 = A	331.408 + 278.649 = U

65.834 + 25.492 = O	8.573 + 4.586 = E
657.712 + 142.971 = C	531.754 + 289.687 = T
407.318 + 17.269 = W	38.965 + 15.317 = M

To solve the riddle, match the letters to the numbered lines below.

192.414   424.587 13.159 95.083 800.683 91.326 98.129 5.362   54.282 610.057 821.441 20.397

©The Education Center, Inc. • *Target Math Success* • TEC60834 • Key p. 136

Adding mixed decimals to thousandths 31

Freestyle Armadillo

Name _____ Date _____

Add.
Show your work on another sheet of paper.
Color if correct.

$26.148 + 7.327 = 22.475$

$5.239 + 4.567 = 9.792$

$68.214 + 19.357 = 87.571$

$30.743 + 22.681 = 53.424$

$42.146 + 9.144 = 51.290$

$41.804 + 6.027 = 102.074$

$54.653 + 75.195 = 128.648$

$12.074 + 7.888 = 19.962$

$97.381 + 80.996 = 178.377$

$123.524 + 16.356 = 139.88$

$13.467 + 7.096 = 20.563$

$506.751 + 9.237 = 515.998$

Adding mixed decimals to thousandths

Orange Outing

Name _____ Date _____

Add.
Show your work.

Why didn't the orange cross the road?

168.5**0** + 1.24 = B	41.67 + 3.7 = I	31.7 + 2.549 = C
59.62 + 4.099 = E	5 + 6.05 = T	88.4 + 73.51 = A

208.87 + 2.2 = S	346.1 + 50.334 = R	54.22 + 8.5 = U	519.253 + 443.6 = E

16.74 + 5.479 = I	6,816.4 + 629.54 = E	7.175 + 6.83 = A	61.476 + 12.93 = C	262.5 + 8.796 = O	72.93 + 78.9 = U
6.12 + 1.982 = O	515.18 + 94.5 = N	91.29 + 18 = U	3,951.4 + 795.98 = F	700.148 + 23.65 = T	49.17 + 28.7 = J

To solve the riddle, match the letters to the numbered lines below.

169.74 63.719 34.249 14.005 151.83 211.07 962.853   45.37 11.05   396.434 161.91 609.68

!

8.102 62.72 723.798   271.296 4,747.38   77.87 109.29 22.219 74.406 7,445.94

©The Education Center, Inc. • *Target Math Success* • TEC60834 • Key p. 136

Using equivalent decimals to add mixed decimals to thousandths

What's for Lunch?

Name _____ Date _____

Add.
Show your work on another sheet of paper.
Color the answer to reveal the path to the seal's lunch.

6.18 + 7.035 =	1.3215	132.15	13.215	1,321.5
57.623 + 81.77 =	13.9393	139.393	1,393.93	13,939.3
13.5 + 416.55 =	4,300.5	43.005	430.05	4.3005
211.533 + 153 =	3.64533	3,645.33	36.4533	364.533
86.7 + 15.902 =	1,026.02	10.2602	1.02602	102.602
492.43 + 68.6 =	5.6103	5,610.3	561.03	56.103
15.2 + 20.94 =	361.4	36.14	0.3614	3.614
93.861 + 107.14 =	201.001	20.1001	2,010.01	21,010.1
3.333 + 16.7 =	2.0033	20.033	200.33	0.20033
119.54 + 95.095 =	2.14635	21.4635	214.635	2,146.35
678.075 + 52.25 =	73,032.5	7,303.25	730.325	73.0325
724.2 + 37 =	76.12	7.612	761.2	0.7612
80.95 + 13.2 =	9.415	94.15	9,415	0.9415
5.147 + 2.3 =	7,447	7.447	74.47	744.7

"Cell-ebrities"

Name _____ Date _____

Add.
Show your work on another sheet of paper.
Write each answer in the magic square. The sum of
each row and column should equal 350.

1) 3.307 + 5.08 =

2) 83.72 + 2.4 =

3) 158.3 + 63.346 =

4) 28.74 + 5.107 =

5) 138.035 + 10.43 =

6) 7.428 + 8.72 =

7) 12.36 + 23.947 =

8) 58.68 + 90.4 =

9) 68.7 + 3.08 =

10) 170.855 + 21.39 =

11) 14.57 + 24.131 =

12) 38.004 + 9.27 =

13) 35.51 + 85.858 =

14) 46.337 + 9.15 =

15) 9.94 + 43.406 =

16) 104.8 + 14.999 =

Using equivalent decimals to add mixed decimals to thousandths

Weather Watch

Name _____ Date _____

Read.
Solve.
Show your work.
Write the answer in the blank.

---

1. Last year in Wetville, it rained 5.73 inches in November and 6.45 inches in December. What was the total rainfall for the two-month period?

   _____ inches

2. On a hot summer day in Sweatown, the average temperature is 98.2°F. If the temperature rises 6.3°F over the average, how hot is it?

   _____°F

---

3. In Windy City, the wind speed was 9.2 miles per hour on Monday and 8.8 miles per hour on Wednesday. What was the total wind speed?

   _____ miles per hour

4. On Friday, it was 28.2°F in Snowville. It warmed up 4.3°F on Tuesday. What was the temperature in Snowville on Tuesday?

   _____°F

---

5. Last year in Winterland it snowed 21.85 centimeters in December and 17.49 centimeters in January. How much did it snow in December and January?

   _____ centimeters

6. Tempie played in the snow too long and caught a winter cold. His temperature was 3.2°F above normal. If normal is 98.6°F, what was Tempie's temperature?

   _____°F

Friends at the Food Court

Name _____ Date _____

Read.
Solve.
Show your work.
Write the answer in the blank.

1. Pepper O. Nee bought a grilled chicken combo for lunch. It cost $4.59. She also bought a cherry slush for $1.67. How much did Pepper spend in all?

   $ _____

2. Pepper's best friend, Olive, bought a taco salad for $5.39 and a medium soda for $1.26. How much did Olive's lunch cost in all?

   $ _____

3. Pepper's sister bought a double cheeseburger for $3.89. Her french fries cost $1.39. How much did Pepper's sister spend in all?

   $ _____

4. Pepper spent $8.45 on food at the mall. Pepper's brother and sister spent $7.01 on their food. How much in all did Pepper, her brother, and her sister spend on food?

   $ _____

5. Pepper's brother spent five dollars at the arcade. Then he bought a slice of pizza for $1.73. How much did Pepper's brother spend in all?

   $ _____

6. Pepper's cousin ordered the chicken stir-fry. It cost $4.85. He also bought a bottle of water for two dollars. How much did Pepper's cousin spend all together?

   $ _____

7. Pepper and Olive each bought cookies after lunch. Pepper's cookie cost $2.19 and Olive's cost $1.38. How much did their cookies cost in all?

   $ _____

8. Pepper's cousin bought an ice-cream cone for $2.46. He also bought a pack of gum for $1.87. How much did Pepper's cousin spend on ice cream and gum?

   $ _____

Fiddler Crab Quartet

Name _____ Date _____

Read.
Solve each problem on a separate sheet of paper.
Write the answer in the blank.

1. Otto practices his viola for 4.5 hours a day. Helen practices her violin for 4.33 hours a day. How many hours a day do they practice in all?

_____ hours

2. Lenny has two favorite songs. "Waves" lasts 13.42 minutes. "Grains of Sand" lasts 7.125 minutes. How many minutes will it take Lenny to play both of his favorite songs?

_____ minutes

3. Karen and Otto both like to play "Under the Dock of the Bay." It lasts 21.383 minutes. Karen also loves to play "Quad," which lasts 4.25 minutes. How many minutes will it take Karen to play both songs?

_____ minutes

4. It takes Helen 83.567 minutes to play all of her favorite songs. Lenny, Karen, and Otto can play their favorites in 46.3 minutes. If Helen, Lenny, Karen, and Otto played all of their favorite songs, how long would it take?

_____ minutes

5. If Karen's cello weighs 5.65 pounds and its case weighs 9 pounds, how many pounds do her cello and its case weigh together?

_____ pounds

6. Helen took private violin lessons for 3.72 years. She attended violin classes at school for 4.5 years. For how long has Helen been learning to play the violin?

_____ years

Subtracting Decimals

Subtracting Decimals
Table of Contents

Parent Communication and Student Checkups

*See pages 112–117 for corresponding parent communications and student checkups (mini tests) for these skills.

Apple Delight!

Name _____   Date _____

Subtract.
Show your work.

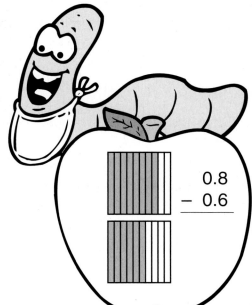

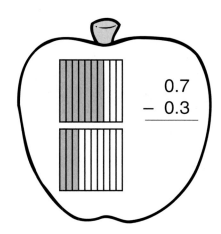
$$\begin{array}{r} 0.7 \\ -\ 0.3 \\ \hline \end{array}$$

$$\begin{array}{r} 0.9 \\ -\ 0.1 \\ \hline \end{array}$$

$$\begin{array}{r} 0.8 \\ -\ 0.6 \\ \hline \end{array}$$

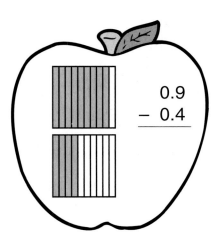
$$\begin{array}{r} 0.9 \\ -\ 0.4 \\ \hline \end{array}$$

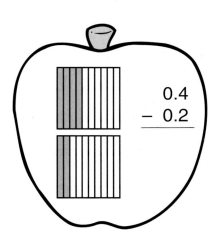
$$\begin{array}{r} 0.4 \\ -\ 0.2 \\ \hline \end{array}$$

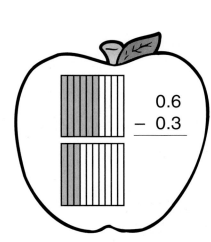
$$\begin{array}{r} 0.6 \\ -\ 0.3 \\ \hline \end{array}$$

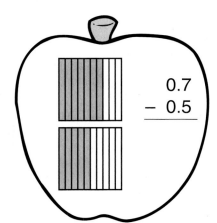
$$\begin{array}{r} 0.7 \\ -\ 0.5 \\ \hline \end{array}$$

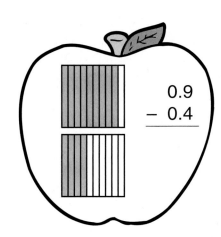
$$\begin{array}{r} 0.9 \\ -\ 0.4 \\ \hline \end{array}$$

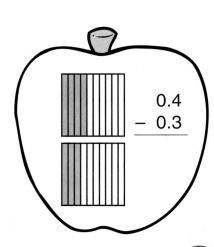
$$\begin{array}{r} 0.4 \\ -\ 0.3 \\ \hline \end{array}$$

Drumming Dragon

Name _____ Date _____

Subtract.
Show your work.

$$1.2 - 0.5$$

$$1.5 - 0.8$$

$$2.4 - 1.7$$

$$1.2 - 0.6$$

$$2.1 - 0.9$$

$$3.5 - 1.6$$

Subtracting mixed decimals to tenths

Stop and Smell the Roses

Name _____ Date _____

Subtract.
Show your work.
Write each answer in the magic square.
The sum of each row and column should equal 300.

  1.
$$\begin{array}{r} 7.5 \\ -\ 3.6 \\ \hline \end{array}$$

  2.
$$\begin{array}{r} 12.2 \\ -\ 4.8 \\ \hline \end{array}$$

  3.
$$\begin{array}{r} 50.3 \\ -\ 19.4 \\ \hline \end{array}$$

  4.
$$\begin{array}{r} 322.6 \\ -\ 64.8 \\ \hline \end{array}$$

  5.
$$\begin{array}{r} 170.2 \\ -\ 5.9 \\ \hline \end{array}$$

  6.
$$\begin{array}{r} 25.1 \\ -\ 16.4 \\ \hline \end{array}$$

7.
$$\begin{array}{r} 480.3 \\ -\ 358.9 \\ \hline \end{array}$$

8.
$$\begin{array}{r} 63.4 \\ -\ 57.8 \\ \hline \end{array}$$

9. $826.1 - 745.9 =$

10. $254.0 - 121.9 =$

11. $99.1 - 24.9 =$

12. $108.2 - 94.7 =$

13. $512.4 - 460.8 =$

14. $961.3 - 809.5 =$

15. $79.4 - 5.9 =$

16. $745.0 - 721.9 =$

Subtracting mixed decimals to tenths **45**

The Cat's Out of the Bag

Name _____   Date _____

Subtract.
Show your work.

(A)   9.84
    − 2.43

(T)   24.63
    − 13.48

(Y)   87.52
    − 35.47

(H)   17.94
    − 6.26

(S)   34.23
    − 3.49

(I)   9.74
    − 5.05

(T)   21.36
    − 18.47

(E)   43.77
    − 8.42

(H)   84.03
    − 62.74

(E)   65.72
    − 4.38

(V)   7.04
    − 3.99

(E)   64.22
    − 27.61

(N)   93.42
    − 13.76

(T)   25.18
    − 11.79

(K)   74.88
    − 9.99

(!)   32.47
    − 28.55

What do cats have that no other animals have?
To solve the riddle, match the letters above to the numbered lines below.

____ ____ ____ ____   ____ ____ ____ ____
11.15 21.29 36.61 52.05   11.68 7.41 3.05 35.35

____ ____ ____ ____ ____ ____ ____ ____
64.89 4.69 13.39 2.89 61.34 79.66 30.74 3.92

Subtracting mixed decimals to hundredths

Balancing Act

Name _____ Date _____

Subtract.
Show your work on another sheet of paper.
Color by the code.

$35.24 - 4.13 =$

$87.15 - 32.95 =$

$94.82 - 12.01 =$ $88.95 - 13.23 =$

$55.68 - 3.54 =$ $9.77 - 2.52 =$ $79.37 - 24.16 =$

$94.23 - 17.82 =$

$75.84 - 64.51 =$ $66.44 - 25.34 =$ $9.24 - 4.69 =$

$48.04 - 10.83 =$ $37.69 - 12.69 =$ $38.89 - 7.71 =$

$20.45 - 9.23 =$ $57.79 - 5.18 =$ $20.56 - 9.15 =$

$98.74 - 6.42 =$ $85.83 - 9.42 =$

$91.81 - 20.41 =$

$46.79 - 19.67 =$

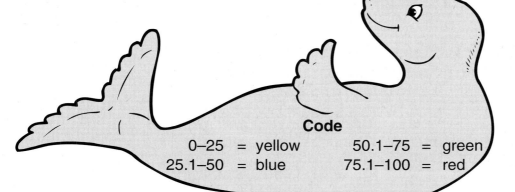

Code

0–25 = yellow	50.1–75 = green
25.1–50 = blue	75.1–100 = red

Subtracting mixed decimals to hundredths   47

Daydreamin'

Name _____   Date _____

Subtract.
Show your work on another sheet of paper.
Cross off the matching answer on the camel.

$5.92 – $2.28 = _____

42.30 – 5.67 = _____

8.06 – 3.19 = _____

500.25 – 0.67 = _____

$96.51 – $61.23 = _____

7.11 – 6.88 = _____

412.34 – 198.25 = _____

$915.45 – $67.09 = _____

3.76 – 2.87 = _____

$26.31 – $15.19 = _____

73.84 – 9.56 = _____

121.41 – 65.32 = _____

57.30 – 36.59 = _____

$4.12 – $2.08 = _____

69.73 – 21.54 = _____

304.67 – 40.49 = _____

$273.23 – $164.75 = _____

80.60 – 17.87 = _____

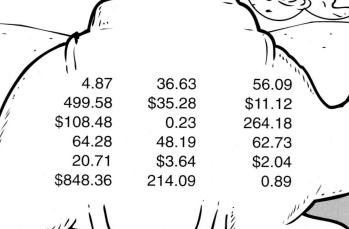

4.87	36.63	56.09
499.58	$35.28	$11.12
$108.48	0.23	264.18
64.28	48.19	62.73
20.71	$3.64	$2.04
$848.36	214.09	0.89

Lily Pad Leap

Name _____ Date _____

Subtract.
Color if correct to show the path to the other side of
the pond.

$$\begin{array}{r} 24.283 \\ - 13.962 \\ \hline 10.321 \end{array}$$ **Start**

$$\begin{array}{r} 6.324 \\ - 3.572 \\ \hline 2.752 \end{array}$$

$$\begin{array}{r} 9.46 \\ - 8.34 \\ \hline 1.22 \end{array}$$

$$\begin{array}{r} 9.28 \\ - 0.89 \\ \hline 8.38 \end{array}$$

$$\begin{array}{r} 67.248 \\ - 23.672 \\ \hline 44.576 \end{array}$$

$$\begin{array}{r} 8.98 \\ - 2.64 \\ \hline 6.34 \end{array}$$

$$\begin{array}{r} 5.742 \\ - 3.308 \\ \hline 2.464 \end{array}$$

$$\begin{array}{r} 81.164 \\ - 7.286 \\ \hline 73.878 \end{array}$$

$$\begin{array}{r} 2.48 \\ - 1.59 \\ \hline 0.89 \end{array}$$

$$\begin{array}{r} 13.274 \\ - 2.681 \\ \hline 10.592 \end{array}$$

$$\begin{array}{r} 13.825 \\ - 9.146 \\ \hline 4.679 \end{array}$$

$$\begin{array}{r} 95.271 \\ - 37.405 \\ \hline 56.066 \end{array}$$

$$\begin{array}{r} 36.808 \\ - 24.743 \\ \hline 10.065 \end{array}$$

$$\begin{array}{r} 38.279 \\ - 8.425 \\ \hline 25.964 \end{array}$$

$$\begin{array}{r} 26.823 \\ - 11.453 \\ \hline 15.370 \end{array}$$

$$\begin{array}{r} 40.909 \\ - 18.707 \\ \hline 22.002 \end{array}$$

$$\begin{array}{r} 57.145 \\ - 36.928 \\ \hline 30.217 \end{array}$$

$$\begin{array}{r} 80.559 \\ - 35.257 \\ \hline 55.302 \end{array}$$

Finish

$$\begin{array}{r} 91.146 \\ - 22.234 \\ \hline 68.912 \end{array}$$

$$\begin{array}{r} 25.176 \\ - 17.342 \\ \hline 7.834 \end{array}$$

$$\begin{array}{r} 86.205 \\ - 29.305 \\ \hline 56.900 \end{array}$$

Have a (Beach) Ball!

Name _____ Date _____

Subtract.
Show your work.
The first one has been started
for you.

14.5
− 3.07
_____

36.6
− 25.11
_____

9.75
− 6.4
_____

18.8**0**
− 4.51
_____

24.5
− 3.23
_____

12.48
− 1.3
_____

8.74
− 8.1
_____

65.84
− 4.6
_____

224.7
− 124.62
_____

5.8
− 4.61
_____

40.7
− 20.53
_____

16.42
− 6.2
_____

742.9
− 31.75
_____

180.63
− 10.4
_____

Using equivalent decimals to subtract mixed decimals to hundredths

Colorful Caterpillar

Name _____ Date _____

Subtract.
Show your work on another sheet of paper.
Color by the code.

12.4 – 3.27 = _____ B

63.8 – 38.52 = _____ P

135.73 – 124.2 = _____ G

31.2 – 1.65 = _____ B

290.4 – 184.66 = _____ R

208.25 – 3.6 = _____ B

25.4 – 1.37 = _____ G

378.46 – 259.2 = _____ P

21.3 – 15.28 = _____ P

17.9 – 10.31 = _____ O

24.63 – 15.4 = _____ R

40.7 – 38.11 = _____ Y

376.8 – 283.59 = _____ O

64.1 – 21.34 = _____ O

425.78 – 5.5 = _____ Y

119.2 – 84.15 = _____ G

35.8 – 29.46 = _____ B

57.39 – 42.9 = _____ O

346.5 – 273.32 = _____ Y

152.6 – 140.78 = _____ P

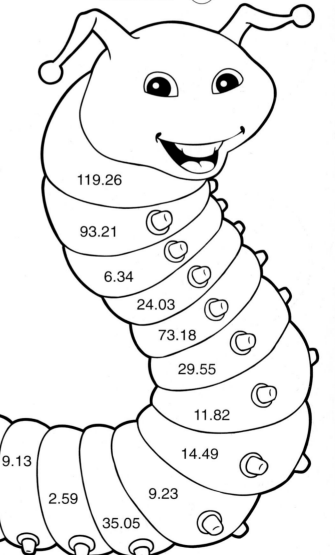

"Salamand-air"

Name _____ Date _____

Subtract.
Show your work on another sheet.
Cross off each matching answer in the answer bank.

86.06 – 13.4 = _____   88.99 – 79.3 = _____

267.18 – 40.392 = _____   635.45 – 244.551 = _____

413.2 – 110.751 = _____   48.578 – 32.21 = _____

65.203 – 19.81 = _____   392.37 – 9.462 = _____

43.845 – 25.66 = _____   17.119 – 10.9 = _____

920.375 – 51.14 = _____   53.46 – 12.613 = _____

34.62 – 32.541 = _____

71.05 – 8.275 = _____

79.46 – 28.056 = _____

26.834 – 7.05 = _____

Look at me, Grandpa!

Answer Bank

390.899	51.404	302.449	18.185
2.079	6.219	9.69	62.775
45.393	72.66	382.908	16.368
869.235	19.784	226.788	40.847

Using equivalent decimals to subtract mixed decimals to thousandths

Searching High and Low

Name _____   Date _____

Subtract.
Show your work on another sheet.

What did the leaf say about looking for his lost ticket to the garden show?

3.02 − 2.7 = _____ Ⓛ

27.49 − 3.5 = _____ Ⓔ

16.15 − 8.394 = _____ Ⓣ

109.77 − 53.8 = _____ Ⓘ

211.8 − 73.91 = _____ Ⓝ

854.71 − 415.453 = _____ Ⓤ

429.43 − 78.8 = _____ Ⓔ

106.75 − 85.254 = _____ Ⓛ

99.658 − 89.88 = _____ Ⓤ

11.2 − 9.279 = _____ Ⓔ

41.57 − 26.063 = _____ Ⓐ

80.3 − 76.741 = _____ Ⓝ

85.6 − 76.29 = _____ Ⓝ

6.873 − 3.49 = _____ Ⓣ

96.102 − 72.13 = _____ Ⓞ

2.82 − 2.409 = _____ Ⓓ

115.27 − 61.3 = _____ Ⓡ

29.4 − 27.29 = _____ Ⓕ

726.6 − 560.72 = _____ Ⓞ

38.23 − 20.085 = _____ Ⓛ

643.71 − 176.5 = _____ Ⓝ

36.04 − 4.8 = _____ Ⓢ

To solve the riddle, write the circled letter in the matching blank.

____ , ____ ____   ____ ____ ____ ____
55.97 0.32 21.496 18.145 350.63 15.507 2.11

____ ____   ____ ____ ____ ____ ____
137.89 23.972 31.24 3.383 165.88 3.559 23.99

____ ____ ____ ____ ____ ____ ____ ____ !
9.778 467.21 7.756 439.257 53.97 9.31 1.921 0.411

Using equivalent decimals to subtract mixed decimals to thousandths **53**

Meeting at the Movies

Name _____ Date _____

Read.
Solve.
Show your work.
Write the answer in the blank.

TICKETS

1. It costs $8.25 to go to the movies in the evening. One ticket to the afternoon show only costs $4.50. How much can Macy save by going to the movies in the afternoon instead of in the evening?

   _____

2. Morris has $10.37. If he buys a ticket to the afternoon show for $4.50, how much will he have left?

   _____

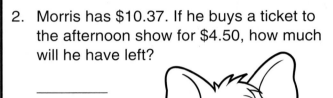

3. Mel has $9.52. If she spends $4.50 on her ticket, how much will she have left?

   _____

4. Max found $3.73 in his backpack. How much more money does he need to buy a $4.50 ticket to the afternoon show?

   _____

5. Max, Mel, Macy, and Morris are meeting in the afternoon to watch the latest episode of *M-Men!* All together, Max, Mel, Macy, and Morris have $35.64. Their tickets cost $18.40. How much money do they have left?

   _____

6. If Max, Mel, Macy, and Morris had gone to the evening showing instead of the afternoon show, their tickets would have cost $33.00. How much of their $35.64 would they have had left?

   _____

Race Day

Name _____ Date _____

Read.
Solve each problem on another sheet of paper.
Write the answer in the blank.

On your mark...

1. Gail swam the first lap in 1.89 seconds. She swam the second lap in 1.6 seconds. How much faster did Gail swim the second lap?

   _____ seconds

2. The distance for race one was 19.3 inches. The distance for race two was 6.54 inches. How much longer was the first race?

   _____ inches

3. Gills won the backstroke by 1.7 seconds. Goldy won the butterfly by 1.23 seconds. How much closer was Goldy's race?

   _____ seconds

4. Goldy's time for the around-the-bowl race was 2.86 minutes. Gary's time was 3.4 minutes. How much longer did it take Gary to swim around the bowl?

   _____ minutes

5. Gary swam the last race in 8.79 seconds. There was a timing error, so the judges deducted 1.2 seconds from Gary's time. What was his final time?

   _____ seconds

Goldfin Swim Club

Story problems: using equivalent decimals to subtract mixed decimals 55

Recycleton, USA

Name _____ Date _____

Read.
Solve each problem on another sheet of paper.
Write the answer on the blank provided.

1. The recycling center has collected 515.6 tons of paper this year. Last year, the center collected 482.75 tons. How much more paper has been collected this year?

   _____ tons

2. During the creek cleanup, 3,200.562 pounds of trash were cleaned up. Volunteers sorted out 853.78 pounds of the trash for recycling. How many pounds of trash were left?

   _____ pounds

3. This month, 36.71 percent of the town recycled milk cartons. Last month, 23.5 percent did. What is the difference?

   _____ percent

4. Of the 2,500 pounds of aluminum cans sold in Recycleton, 1,276.33 pounds were recycled. How many pounds were not recycled?

   _____ pounds

5. Of the plastic recycled this year, 71.83 percent was type 2 plastic. Type 1 plastic made up 16.079 percent. What is the difference?

   _____ percent

6. It cost 15.8 million dollars to run the recycling center last year. This year, it has cost 14.259 million dollars. How much less has it cost this year?

   _____ million dollars

Multiplying Decimals

Multiplying Decimals
Table of Contents

Parent Communication and Student Checkups

*See pages 118–125 for corresponding parent communications and student checkups (mini tests) for these skills.

Emergency!

Name _____   Date _____

Add.
Show your work.
To solve the riddle, color the matching letter.

0.7 x 3	315 x 0.2	0.9 x 8	46 x 0.4	0.2 x 9
37 x 0.5	0.3 x 8	116 x 0.7	0.5 x 5	12 x 0.4
25 x 0.8	73 x 0.6	0.6 x 6	44 x 0.9	0.4 x 3

Why did the book go to the hospital?

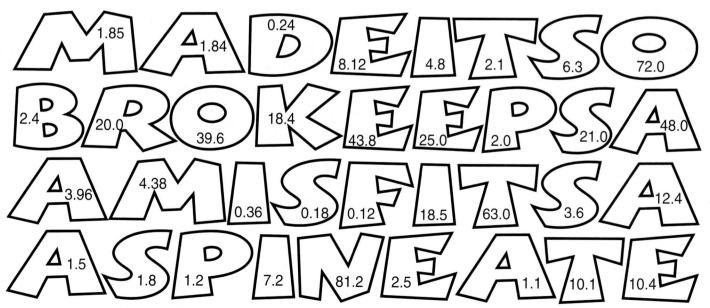

M 1.85 A 1.84 D 0.24 E 8.12 I 4.8 T 2.1 S 6.3 O 72.0

B 2.4 R 20.0 O 39.6 K 18.4 E 43.8 E 25.0 P 2.0 S 21.0 A 48.0

A 3.96 M 4.38 I 0.36 S 0.18 F 0.12 I 18.5 T 63.0 S 3.6 A 12.4

A 1.5 S 1.8 P 1.2 I 7.2 N 81.2 E 2.5 A 1.1 T 10.1 E 10.4

"En-light-ening" Conversation

Name _____   Date _____

Multiply.
Show your work.
To solve the riddle, match the letters to the numbered lines below.

0.12	0.65	$0.53	0.33
x 6	x 6	x 3	x 8
= H	= I	= S	= E

$0.23	123	402	325
x 16	x 0.14	x 0.21	x 0.43
= O	= T	= N	= L

0.93	0.82	$0.91	0.18
x 6	x 4	x 7	x 5
= T	= G	= T	= O

0.47	$0.75	264	116
x 5	x 4	x 0.13	x 0.29
= T	= U	= O	= G

What did one candle say to the other candle?

_____ _____ _____ _____ , _____ _____   _____ _____ _____
139.75   2.64 $6.37 $1.59   33.64   34.32 $3.68 $3.00   17.22

_____ _____ _____ _____ _____ _____ _____ !
5.58   0.90   84.42   3.90   3.28   0.72   2.35

©The Education Center, Inc. • *Target Math Success* • TEC60834 • Key p. 139

60 *Multiplying decimals to hundredths by whole numbers*

Banana Bandit

Name _____ Date _____

Multiply.
Show your work on another sheet of paper.
Color yellow if correct to show how many bananas the monkey stole.

0.6 x 6 = 0.36

0.21 x 5 = 10.5

0.85 x 6 = 0.51

412 x 0.7 = 28.84

0.86 x 3 = 2.58

620 x 0.9 = 55.8

242 x 0.2 = 48.4

0.4 x 8 = 3.2

0.47 x 58 = 27.26

99 x 0.8 = 79.2

782 x 0.4 = 31.28

0.76 x 7 = 5.32

58 x 0.5 = 29.0

0.22 x 9 = 19.8

501 x 0.18 = 90.18

0.68 x 7 = 47.6

0.37 x 4 = 1.48

0.29 x 33 = 9.57

0.7 x 3 = 0.21

Buster's Bargains

Name _____   Date _____

Read.
Solve each problem in the space provided.
Write the answer in the blank.

Buster's Barber Shop
TODAY ONLY!
Shave $0.50   Haircut $0.75

1. Today 35 customers got shaves at Buster's Barber Shop. If each customer paid $0.50 for a shave, how much money did Buster make in all? _____

2. Sixty customers got haircuts before lunch. At $0.75 for each cut, how much money did Buster make on haircuts before lunch? _____

3. During the afternoon, 85 customers got haircuts. At $0.75 for each cut, how much money did Buster make on haircuts during the afternoon?

   _____

4. Greg the goat's beard grows 0.68 centimeters a day. How much will his beard grow in all after 3 days?

   _____ centimeters

5. Billy the goat's beard grows 0.7 centimeters a day. How much will his beard grow in all after 14 days? _____ centimeters

6. Bob the cat wanted his hair trimmed 0.5 centimeters. If this amount is trimmed on 12 different visits, how much hair will Buster trim in all? _____ centimeters

Roll It On!

Name _____ Date _____

Read.
Solve each problem on another sheet of paper.
Write the answer in the blank.

1.
Robby Roller adds 0.3 ounces of tint to each gallon of brown paint. How many ounces of tint will he need to add for 65 gallons?

_____ ounces

2.
Tina Tray has 8 gallons of paint. If she adds 0.72 ounces of tint to each gallon, how much tint will she add in all?

_____ ounces

3.
Robby needs to add 0.49 ounces of tint to each gallon of red paint. How many ounces of tint will he need for 12 gallons?

_____ ounces

4.
Tina has 235 gallons of green paint. If she adds 0.6 ounces of tint to each gallon, how much tint will she add in all?

_____ ounces

5.
Robby adds 0.8 ounces of tint to each gallon of blue paint. If he tints 500 gallons, how many ounces of tint will he use in all?

_____ ounces

6.
Tina has 47 gallons of purple paint. If she adds 0.26 ounces of tint to each gallon, how much tint will she use in all?

_____ ounces

©The Education Center, Inc. • *Target Math Success* • TEC60834 • Key p. 139

Story Problems: multiplying decimals to hundredths by whole numbers 63

Heard the Skunk's Joke?

Multiply.
Show your work.
Color each shape that contains a correct answer.

$$\begin{array}{r} 0.6 \\ \times\ 0.3 \\ \hline \end{array}$$

$$\begin{array}{r} 0.7 \\ \times\ 0.4 \\ \hline \end{array}$$

$$\begin{array}{r} 0.3 \\ \times\ 0.2 \\ \hline \end{array}$$

$$\begin{array}{r} 0.6 \\ \times\ 0.5 \\ \hline \end{array}$$

$$\begin{array}{r} 0.9 \\ \times\ 0.5 \\ \hline \end{array}$$

$$\begin{array}{r} 0.4 \\ \times\ 0.8 \\ \hline \end{array}$$

$$\begin{array}{r} 0.2 \\ \times\ 0.1 \\ \hline \end{array}$$

$$\begin{array}{r} 0.8 \\ \times\ 0.3 \\ \hline \end{array}$$

$$\begin{array}{r} 0.7 \\ \times\ 0.7 \\ \hline \end{array}$$

$$\begin{array}{r} 0.9 \\ \times\ 0.3 \\ \hline \end{array}$$

$$\begin{array}{r} 0.1 \\ \times\ 0.4 \\ \hline \end{array}$$

$$\begin{array}{r} 0.6 \\ \times\ 0.8 \\ \hline \end{array}$$

0.2 x 0.5 = _____   0.7 x 0.5 = _____   0.2 x 0.7 = _____

0.9 x 0.4 = _____   0.4 x 0.4 = _____   0.7 x 0.8 = _____

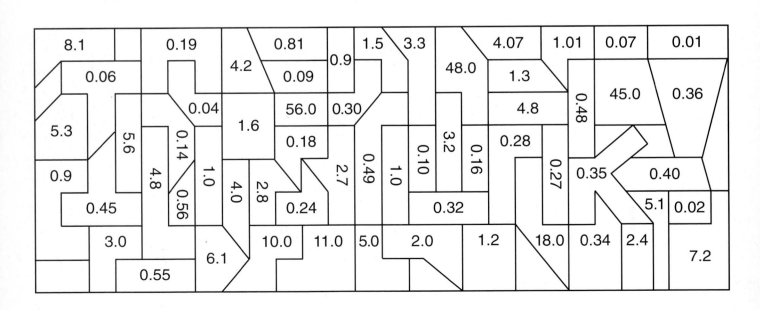

"Snail-athon"

Name _____ Date _____

Multiply.
Show your work.

0.01K!

$$0.57 \times 0.9$$

$$0.32 \times 0.8$$

$$0.16 \times 0.4$$

$$0.28 \times 0.6$$

$$0.43 \times 0.5$$

$$0.71 \times 0.7$$

$$0.89 \times 0.3$$

$$0.64 \times 0.2$$

$$0.07 \times 0.8$$

$$0.95 \times 0.5$$

$$0.39 \times 0.6$$

$$0.52 \times 0.4$$

$$0.61 \times 0.2$$

FINISH

$$0.28 \times 0.9$$

$$0.76 \times 0.8$$

$$0.44 \times 0.7$$

Multiplying decimals to hundredths

65

Bath Time!

Name _____ Date _____

Multiply.
Show your work on another sheet of paper.
Color if correct.
Connect all the colored boxes to draw a path to the finish.

Start

0.12 x 0.91 = 0.1192

0.95 x 0.17 = 0.1616

0.23 x 0.14 = 0.0332

0.68 x 0.84 = 0.5712

0.27 x 0.65 = 0.17525

0.52 x 0.86 = 0.4472

0.73 x 0.49 = 0.3577

0.41 x 0.26 = 1.066

0.76 x 0.32 = 2.432

0.82 x 0.53 = 4.346

Finish

0.39 x 0.72 = 0.2808

0.64 x 0.97 = 62.08

0.94 x 0.38 = 0.3572

0.41 x 0.63 = 0.2583

0.35 x 0.41 = 01.435

0.19 x 0.79 = 0.1501

0.88 x 0.58 = 0.5104

0.97 x 0.25 = 0.2425

Go for the Goal!

Name _____ Date _____

Multiply.
Show your work.
Color the boxes with answers greater than 25 to show the path to the goal.

6.7 x 4	3.7 x 7	9.8 x 9	16.8 x 3
3.4 x 4	1.6 x 2	7.3 x 3	2.3 x 7	8.2 x 5
4.7 x 8	11.7 x 3	12.4 x 6	5.6 x 9	10.4 x 6
13.2 x 2	2.9 x 4	4.5 x 5	3.6 x 3	1.8 x 7
8.6 x 6	7.2 x 5	9.4 x 4		

Finish

Start

Taking It to the Bank

Name _____   Date _____

Multiply.
Show your work.

$6.15 x 4	$3.53 x 7	$9.81 x 9	$26.32 x 2	$2.19 x 5
$7.34 x 8	$8.62 x 5	$5.76 x 3	$10.81 x 6	$6.89 x 4
$30.25 x 7	$1.73 x 2	$6.24 x 8	$4.31 x 9	$2.27 x 3
$12.62 x 4	$3.87 x 6	$5.22 x 3		

Oinkville National Bank

Pennies

Multiplying mixed decimals to hundredths by whole numbers

©The Education Center, Inc. • *Target Math Success* • TEC60834 • Key p. 140

Cooling Off

Name _____ Date _____

Multiply.
Show your work on another sheet of paper.
Cross off each answer on the handle.

5.2 x 4 =

3.9 x 8 =

1.74 x 6 =

3.04 x 2 =

8.7 x 9 =

2.76 x 5 =

1.17 x 3 =

28.8 x 7 =

1.01 x 5 =

7.25 x 6 =

46.3 x 2 =

2.78 x 4 =

3.45 x 8 =

9.21 x 5 =

6.04 x 3 =

8.52 x 7 =

7.03 x 2 =

16.1 x 7 =

18.12
11.12
10.44
201.6
59.64
92.6
20.8
6.08
14.06
78.3
13.8
112.7
31.2
43.5
5.05
3.51
46.05
27.6

Multiplying mixed decimals to hundredths by whole numbers 69

Name _____ Date _____

Multiply.
Color by the code.

Color Code
0–25.00 = green
25.01–50.00 = brown
50.01–75.00 = yellow

The Crooning Crickets

Name _____ Date _____

Read.
Solve each problem on another sheet of paper.
Write the answer in the blank.

The Crooning Crickets—Three Nights Only!

1. Seven friends went to the Crooning Crickets concert. Each ticket cost $9.75. How much did the friends pay for their tickets in all? _____

2. During the concert, Carl bought 3 sodas. Each soda cost $1.98. How much did he pay in all? _____

3. T-shirts were on sale for $21.25 each. Carrie bought 2 T-shirts. How much did she pay in all? _____

4. Carla purchased 4 videos of the band. Each video cost $8.99. How much did she pay in all? _____

5. Cole bought 6 of the band's CDs for his family. Each CD cost $7.48. How much did he pay in all? _____

6. Connie bought 5 posters of the band. Each poster cost $2.35. How much did she pay in all? _____

The Crooning Crickets

Story problems: multiplying mixed decimals to hundredths by whole numbers 71

High Dive

Name _____ Date _____

Read.
Show your work on another sheet of paper.
Write the answer in the blank.

9.25 **9.0** **6.5** **8.25**

All-Ocean High Dive Championship

1. At the All-Ocean High Dive Championship, 5 divers from the Whales each received a score of 9.13. What was the divers' total score? _____

2. On the Seals team, 6 divers each received a score of 8.75. What was the divers' total score? _____

3. Three divers from the Eels each received a score of 6.3. What was the divers' total score? _____

4. In the final round, 2 divers from the Sea Lions each received a score of 9.97. What was the divers' total score? _____

5. On the Sharks team, 8 divers each received a score of 8.9. What was the divers' total score? _____

6. Four divers from the Otters each received a score of 9.5. What was the divers' total score? _____

Story problems: multiplying mixed decimals to hundredths by whole numbers

Prickly Pizza

Name _____   Date _____

Multiply.
Show your work.

5.6	1.4
x 0.3	x 0.5
27.5	**3.3**
x 0.2	x 0.8

31.2	45.8
x 0.9	x 0.6
124.3	**6.7**
x 0.1	x 0.4

82.3	7.1
x 0.7	x 0.9
919.7	**453.6**
x 0.6	x 0.4

6.8	307.2
x 0.5	x 0.3
54.5	**79.4**
x 0.2	x 0.7

Multiplying mixed decimals to tenths 73

Push It!

Name _____   Date _____

Multiply.
Show your work.
Write each answer in the magic square. The sum of each
 row and column should equal 100.

1)   33.92
   x 2.54

2)   4.92
   x 0.35

3)   3.64
   x 3.33

4)   1.884
   x 0.09

5)   11.47
   x 6.52

6)   5.25
   x 4.48

7)   303.69
   x 0.04

8)   97.89
   x 0.24

9)   292.54
   x 0.22

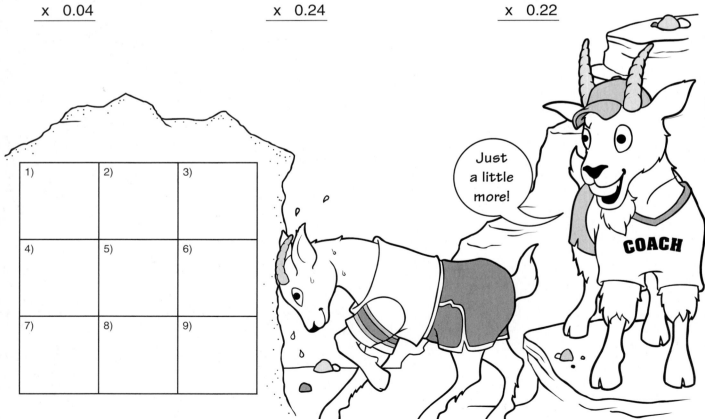

1)	2)	3)
4)	5)	6)
7)	8)	9)

Just a little more!

COACH

Time for a Mint?

Name _____ Date _____

Multiply.
Show your work on another sheet of paper.
Color if correct.

6.3 x 2.5 = 15.75

17.4 x 5.9 = 102.66

50.1 x 3.8 = 19.039

6.07 x 24.9 = 151.143

1.8 x 4.06 = 7.38

93.25 x 0.5 = 46.625

8.42 x 3.33 = 28.0386

2.47 x 3.04 = 7.588

7.5 x 3.29 = 246.75

4.08 x 0.71 = 2.8968

45.5 x 3.3 = 150.15

61.8 x 5.31 = 328.158

170.3 x 9.2 = 1,566.76

351.2 x 6.89 = 24,197.68

104.15 x 35.02 = 3,647.3330

93.62 x 4.68 = 438.1416

27.43 x 81.6 = 238.288

After-Dinner Mints

Multiplying mixed decimals to hundredths

Sunbather

Name _____ Date _____

Multiply.
Show your work.
Color by the code.

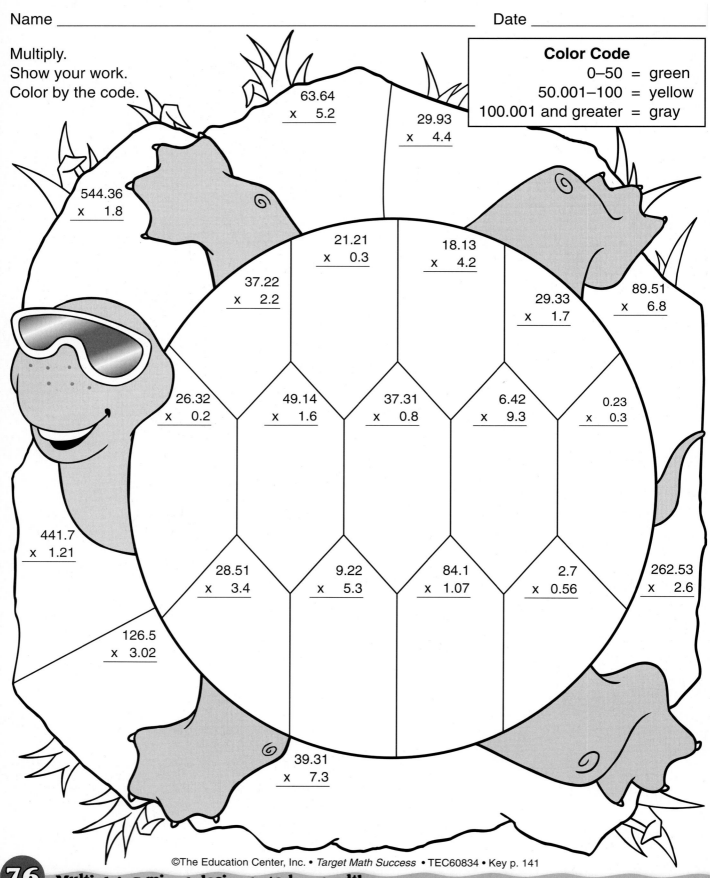

63.64
x 5.2

29.93
x 4.4

544.36
x 1.8

21.21
x 0.3

18.13
x 4.2

37.22
x 2.2

29.33
x 1.7

89.51
x 6.8

26.32
x 0.2

49.14
x 1.6

37.31
x 0.8

6.42
x 9.3

0.23
x 0.3

441.7
x 1.21

28.51
x 3.4

9.22
x 5.3

84.1
x 1.07

2.7
x 0.56

262.53
x 2.6

126.5
x 3.02

39.31
x 7.3

©The Education Center, Inc. • *Target Math Success* • TEC60834 • Key p. 141

Getting a Kick Out of Practice

Name _____ Date _____

Multiply.
Show your work on another sheet.
Color the football that contains the answer.

5.45 x 16.2 = _____

0.31 x 2.8 = _____

7.24 x 3.6 = _____

92.72 x 4.55 = _____

4.08 x 7.2 = _____

73.57 x 9.31 = _____

8.3 x 6.57 = _____

20.49 x 3.36 = _____

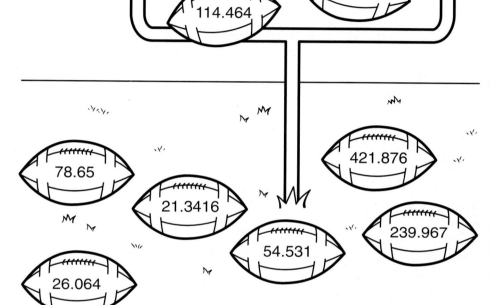

684.9367

0.868

114.464

78.65

421.876

21.3416

239.967

54.531

26.064

11.68 x 9.8 = _____

3.25 x 24.2 = _____

6.91 x 8.44 = _____

4.12 x 5.18 = _____

61.53 x 3.9 = _____

27.5 x 9.14 = _____

29.376

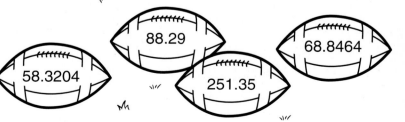

88.29

68.8464

58.3204

251.35

Multiplying mixed decimals to hundredths 77

Creepy, Crawly Cup

Name _____ Date _____

Multiply.
Show your work on another sheet of paper.
Color to show the path to the winner.

Cup Finals

5.073 x 21.2 =	107.5476	106.5475	10,754.76	107.95302
74.415 x 3.72 =	2,768.238	276.82380	276.82387	276.82330
0.862 x 0.56 =	0.48272	48.48272	4.82720	0.48278
29.041 x 32.78 =	95.19638	951.96398	951.96399	95.19639
1.96 x 0.4 =	7.84	0.770	0.784	0.780
83.145 x 21.33 =	17.73482	1,774.48280	1,773.48285	1,775.48280
7.2 x 1.52 =	10.914	109.44	11.014	10.944
68.047 x 36.84 =	25,068.514	250.68514	2,506.85148	2,506.85141
9.431 x 4.3 =	40.5534	4,055.33	39.5564	40.5533
0.936 x 0.52 =	4.86722	0.48678	0.48672	1.4560
0.815 x 2.33 =	0.18989	1.89895	2.11450	0.18988
7.064 x 64.98 =	459.01872	71.01962	45,901.872	459.01852
563.118 x 0.3 =	168.6341	168.9354	168.9341	1,689.354
46.998 x 3.86 =	181.41228	138.41224	18,141.2240	50.35804

78 **Multiplying mixed decimals to thousandths**

Dividing Decimals

Dividing Decimals
Table of Contents

Parent Communication and Student Checkups

*See pages 126–131 for corresponding parent communications and student checkups (mini tests) for these skills.

Going Home to Roost

Name _____ Date _____

Divide.
Show your work.
Color the shapes with answers less than 20 to show the path home.

Start

$4\overline{)66.8}$	$6\overline{)85.2}$

$8\overline{)534.4}$	$2\overline{)389.4}$	$5\overline{)704.5}$	$9\overline{)50.4}$

$7\overline{)582.4}$	$3\overline{)124.8}$	$4\overline{)89.2}$	$8\overline{)14.4}$

$6\overline{)439.2}$	$2\overline{)895.4}$		

Home

Dividing mixed decimals to tenths by whole numbers 81

Underwater Communication

Name _____ Date _____

Divide.
Show your work.

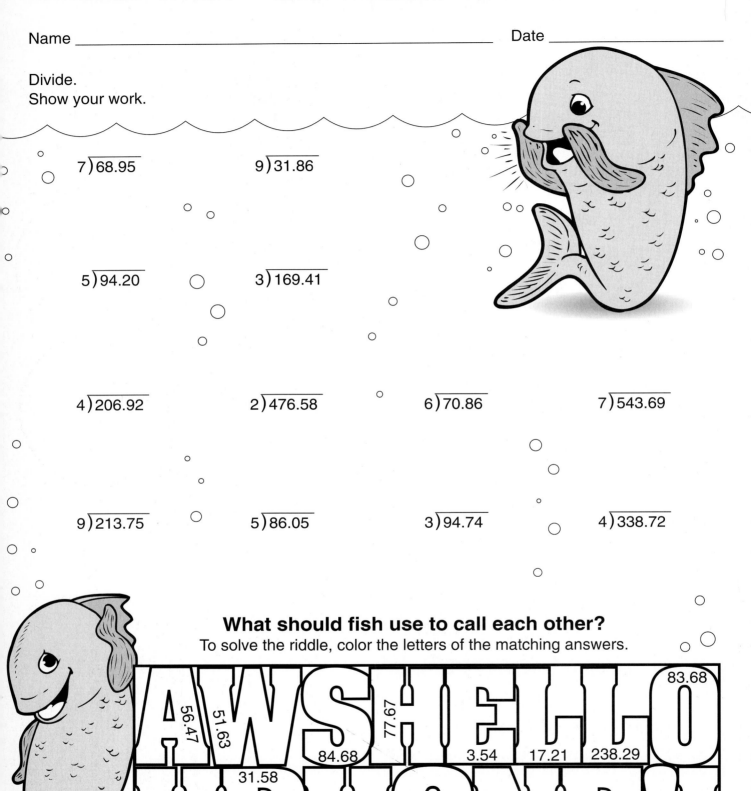

$7 \overline{)68.95}$

$9 \overline{)31.86}$

$5 \overline{)94.20}$

$3 \overline{)169.41}$

$4 \overline{)206.92}$

$2 \overline{)476.58}$

$6 \overline{)70.86}$

$7 \overline{)543.69}$

$9 \overline{)213.75}$

$5 \overline{)86.05}$

$3 \overline{)94.74}$

$4 \overline{)338.72}$

What should fish use to call each other?
To solve the riddle, color the letters of the matching answers.

AWSHELLO
UPHONE!!

56.47 51.63 77.67 83.68
84.68 3.54 17.21 238.29
31.58 11.81
18.84 9.85 8.85
51.63 23.75 51.73

Dividing mixed decimals to hundredths by whole numbers

Got Grapes?

Divide.
Show your work on another sheet of paper.
Color by the code.

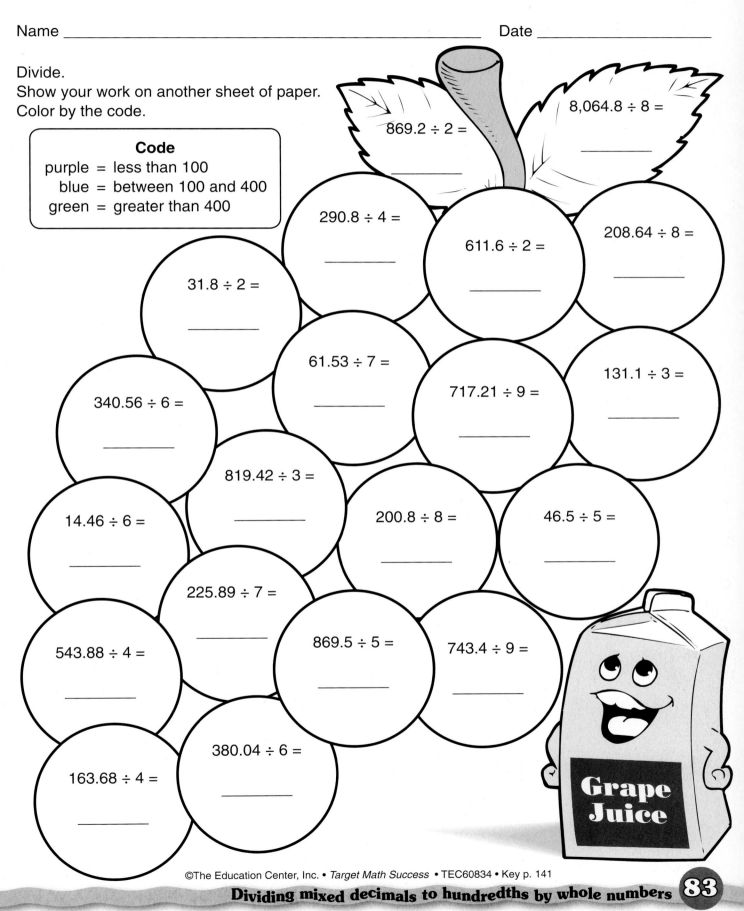

Code
purple = less than 100
blue = between 100 and 400
green = greater than 400

869.2 ÷ 2 = _____

8,064.8 ÷ 8 = _____

290.8 ÷ 4 = _____

611.6 ÷ 2 = _____

208.64 ÷ 8 = _____

31.8 ÷ 2 = _____

61.53 ÷ 7 = _____

717.21 ÷ 9 = _____

131.1 ÷ 3 = _____

340.56 ÷ 6 = _____

819.42 ÷ 3 = _____

14.46 ÷ 6 = _____

200.8 ÷ 8 = _____

46.5 ÷ 5 = _____

225.89 ÷ 7 = _____

543.88 ÷ 4 = _____

869.5 ÷ 5 = _____

743.4 ÷ 9 = _____

380.04 ÷ 6 = _____

163.68 ÷ 4 = _____

Grape
Juice

What Has Four Wheels and Flies?

Name _____   Date _____

Divide.
Show your work.
To solve the riddle, match the letters to the numbered lines below.

(C) 2)18.342   (B) 4)649.916   (A) 6)2.484   (R) 8)75.416

(T) 3)5.988   (E) 5)61.495   (R) 7)34.041   (A) 9)861.435

(G) 2)7.848   (!) 4)10.496   (G) 6)7.644   (U) 8)246.808

(A) 3)45.678   (K) 5)987.655

			0.414			
3.924	15.226	9.427	162.479	95.715	1.274	12.299

1.996	4.863	30.851	9.171	197.531	2.624

Dividing mixed decimals to thousandths by whole numbers

Having a Ball at the Putting Green!

Divide.
Show your work.

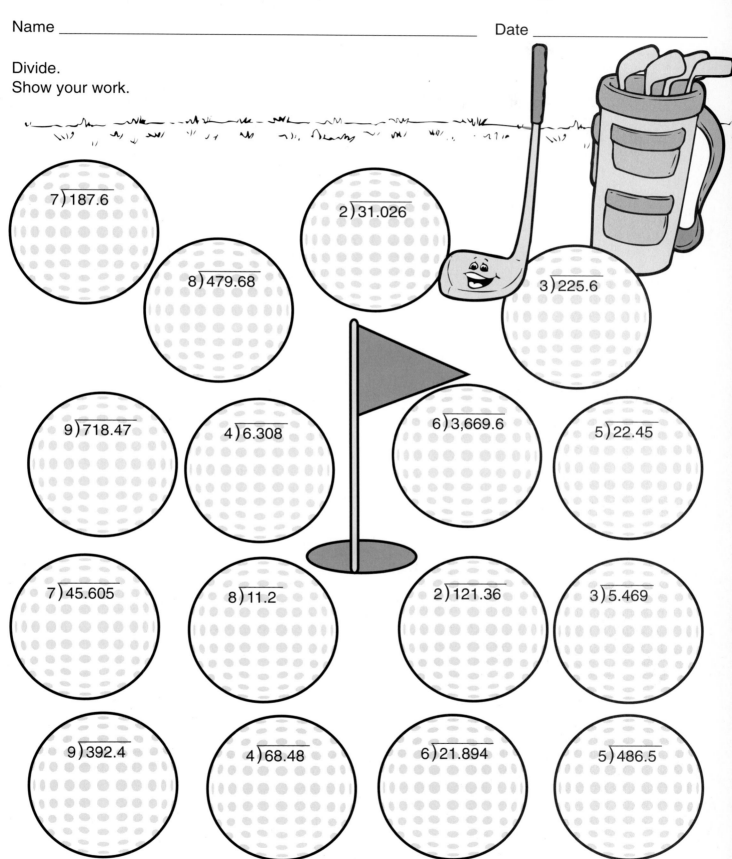

$7 \overline{)187.6}$

$8 \overline{)479.68}$

$2 \overline{)31.026}$

$3 \overline{)225.6}$

$9 \overline{)718.47}$

$4 \overline{)6.308}$

$6 \overline{)3,669.6}$

$5 \overline{)22.45}$

$7 \overline{)45.605}$

$8 \overline{)11.2}$

$2 \overline{)121.36}$

$3 \overline{)5.469}$

$9 \overline{)392.4}$

$4 \overline{)68.48}$

$6 \overline{)21.894}$

$5 \overline{)486.5}$

Dividing mixed decimals to thousandths by whole numbers

85

Close Companions

Divide.
Show your work on another sheet of paper.
Cross off the answers on the keyboard.
Some of the answers will not be crossed off.

5.44 ÷ 4 = _____   14.84 ÷ 7 = _____   10.816 ÷ 4 = _____

129.5 ÷ 5 = _____   6.801 ÷ 3 = _____   78.6 ÷ 6 = _____

54.08 ÷ 8 = _____   149.6 ÷ 2 = _____   35.01 ÷ 9 = _____

29.625 ÷ 3 = _____   43.939 ÷ 7 = _____   87.95 ÷ 5 = _____

60.4 ÷ 4 = _____   73.36 ÷ 2 = _____   882.6 ÷ 6 = _____

8.336 ÷ 8 = _____   73.5 ÷ 5 = _____   64.855 ÷ 7 = _____

2.267	147.1	74.8	9.265	6.76	62.77	36.68		3.89	1.042
14.71	15.1	14.7	3.668	25.9	13.1	9.875		104.2	1.36
6.277						2.12		2.704	17.59

Soup's On!

Name _____ Date _____

Read.
Solve each problem on another sheet of paper.
Write the answer in the blank.

1. Chef Fred sliced 10.8-inch stalks of celery into pieces for his soup. If he cut each stalk into 4 equal pieces, how long was each piece?

_____ inches

2. Fred chopped 8.28-inch slices of bacon into pieces. If he cut each slice into 6 equal pieces, how long was each piece?

_____ inches

3. Fred's assistant cut 6.335-inch chicken strips into chunks. If he cut each strip into 5 equal chunks, how long was each chunk?

_____ inches

4. Fred's assistant also diced 120.6-centimeter strips of potato. If he diced each strip into 9 equal pieces, how long was each piece?

_____ centimeters

5. Chef Fred cut 71.52-centimeter strips of green pepper into pieces. If he cut each strip into 8 equal pieces, how long was each piece?

_____ centimeters

6. Fred also sliced 273.182-centimeter strips of carrot into pieces. If he cut each strip into 7 equal pieces, how long was each piece?

_____ centimeters

Tools of the Trade

Name _____ Date _____

Read.
Solve each problem on another
    sheet of paper.
Write the answer in the blank.

1.

Tess is cutting an 18.276-yard
bolt of fabric into pieces to sew
tablecloths for a party. If she cuts
the fabric into 6 equal pieces,
how long will each piece be?

_____ yards

2.

Tess's husband, Jess, is cutting
a 139.5-foot length of felt to
make banners. If he cuts the felt
into 5 equal pieces, how long
will each piece be?

_____ feet

3.

Tess is cutting a 2.45-meter
length of ribbon to make bows. If
she cuts the ribbon into 7 equal
pieces, how long will each piece
be?

_____ meters

4.

Jess is making chair cushions
from a 9.21-yard bolt of fabric.
If he cuts the fabric into 3 equal
pieces, how long will each piece
be?

_____ yards

5.

Tess is making table napkins
from an 88.2-inch length of fabric. If she cuts the fabric into 9
equal pieces, how long will each
piece be?

_____ inches

6.

Jess is helping Tess make draperies from a 21.088-yard bolt of
fabric. If they cut the fabric into
4 equal pieces, how long will
each piece be?

_____ yards

Story problems: dividing mixed decimals to thousandths by whole numbers

Circus Switcheroo

Name _____   Date _____

Divide.
Show your work.
Write each answer in the magic square.
The sum of each row and column should equal 200.

① $0.6\overline{)36}$ ② $0.5\overline{)35}$ ③ $0.3\overline{)9}$ ④ $0.5\overline{)20}$

⑤ $0.2\overline{)10}$ ⑥ $0.4\overline{)12}$ ⑦ $0.2\overline{)9}$ ⑧ $0.8\overline{)60}$

⑨ $0.7\overline{)49}$ ⑩ $0.2\overline{)4}$ ⑪ $0.2\overline{)7}$ ⑫ $0.4\overline{)30}$

⑬ $0.9\overline{)18}$ ⑭ $0.8\overline{)64}$ ⑮ $0.3\overline{)27}$ ⑯ $0.6\overline{)6}$

Shoot for the Stars

Name _____   Date _____

Divide.
Show your work.

$0.25 \overline{)\ 5}$

$0.36 \overline{)\ 18}$

$0.14 \overline{)\ 56}$

$0.03 \overline{)\ 39}$

$0.05 \overline{)\ 7}$

$0.33 \overline{)\ 66}$

$0.25 \overline{)\ 2}$

$0.28 \overline{)\ 84}$

$0.64 \overline{)\ 16}$

$0.17 \overline{)\ 68}$

$0.22 \overline{)\ 33}$

$0.27 \overline{)\ 81}$

$0.06 \overline{)\ 3}$

$0.15 \overline{)\ 75}$

$0.24 \overline{)\ 96}$

Dividing whole numbers by decimals to hundredths

I'll Have the Cheese, Please

Name _____ Date _____

Divide.
Show your work on another sheet of paper.
Color if correct. Connect the colored boxes to draw a path to the finish.

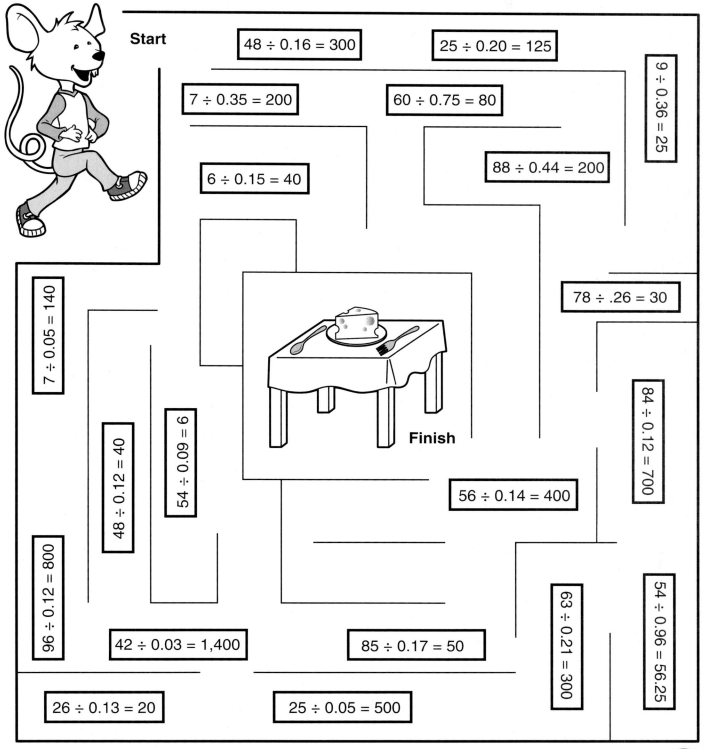

Start

$48 \div 0.16 = 300$

$25 \div 0.20 = 125$

$9 \div 0.36 = 25$

$7 \div 0.35 = 200$

$60 \div 0.75 = 80$

$6 \div 0.15 = 40$

$88 \div 0.44 = 200$

$78 \div .26 = 30$

$7 \div 0.05 = 140$

$84 \div 0.12 = 700$

Finish

$48 \div 0.12 = 40$

$54 \div 0.09 = 6$

$56 \div 0.14 = 400$

$96 \div 0.12 = 800$

$63 \div 0.21 = 300$

$54 \div 0.96 = 56.25$

$42 \div 0.03 = 1,400$

$85 \div 0.17 = 50$

$26 \div 0.13 = 20$

$25 \div 0.05 = 500$

Dividing whole numbers by decimals to hundredths 91

Pinching Pennies

Name _____ Date _____

Read.
Solve each problem on another sheet of paper.
Write the answer in the blank.

1. Pete is saving $0.45 each week to buy a video game that costs $9.00. How many weeks will he have to save?

_____ weeks

2. Each week, Patsy saves $0.75 so she can purchase a shirt that costs $15.00. How many weeks will she have to save?

_____ weeks

3. Pablo is saving $0.12 a day to buy a book. If the book costs $6.00, how many days will he have to save to have enough money to buy the book?

_____ days

4. Each week, Patrick sets aside $0.32 from his allowance. He wants to buy a game that costs $16.00. How many weeks will he have to save?

_____ weeks

5. Paige saves $0.80 each month to buy a CD that costs $12.00. How many months will she have to save in order to buy the CD?

_____ months

6. Each week, Parker saves $0.25 so he can buy a movie that costs $8.00. How many weeks will he have to save?

_____ weeks

7. Paula saves $0.30 a day so she can buy a DVD that costs $18.00. How many days will she need to save in order to have enough to buy the DVD?

_____ days

OINK-MART

Story problems: dividing whole numbers by decimals to hundredths

Talk of the Pond

Name _____   Date _____

Divide.
Show your work.

She's here!

$1.2\overline{)33.6}$

$3.5\overline{)8.4}$

$4.6\overline{)66.7}$

$8.1\overline{)153.9}$

$2.6\overline{)6.5}$

$62.5\overline{)1,127.5}$

$41.2\overline{)30.9}$

$18.8\overline{)136.3}$

$7.2\overline{)592.2}$

$5.6\overline{)85.4}$

$9.6\overline{)730.8}$

$0.5\overline{)48.6}$

Dividing mixed decimals to tenths **93**

A Friendly Rematch

Name _____ Date _____

Divide.
Show your work.
Cross off each matching answer on the grass.
Some answers will not be crossed off.

$2.46 \overline{)\ 29.52}$

$1.85 \overline{)\ 60.31}$

$3.15 \overline{)\ 15.12}$

$8.75 \overline{)\ 47.81}$

$4.31 \overline{)\ 2{,}693.75}$

$7.35 \overline{)\ 1{,}919.82}$

$4.11 \overline{)\ 2{,}207.07}$

$9.52 \overline{)\ 6{,}797.28}$

$5.98 \overline{)\ 1{,}034.54}$

4.8

173

261.2

513   2.848

625   316   32.6

          5.464

START

714   125

12

537

Hot on the Ice-Cream Trail

Name _____ Date _____

Divide.
Show your work on another sheet of paper.
Color if correct to show the path to the ice-cream truck.

Start

$5 $1.25)$6.25	115 3.41)392.15

71.5 6.32)451.88	.265 4.12)109.18	$6.65 3.33)$2,221.11	3.45 4.06)140.07
31 7.14)221.34	$265 $2.47)$654.55	.277 1.58)43.45	23.5 5.43)124.89
$.053 $8.25)$437.25	161 5.61)903.21	1.27 2.56)440.32	403.3 3.71)1,495.13

Finish

44.3 6.65)288.61	$65 $2.55)$165.75	$25 $4.95)$123.75

Dividing mixed decimals to hundredths

95

Spelling Surprise

Name _____   Date _____

Divide.
Show your work on another sheet of paper.
Write the answer on the blank.
To solve the riddle, color the letters that have matching answers.

What word is always spelled incorrectly?

396.36 ÷ 1.08 = _____

50.88 ÷ 4.24 = _____   982.52 ÷ 8.47 = _____

31.28 ÷ 7.36 = _____   1,443.18 ÷ 3.59 = _____

52.44 ÷ 9.12 = _____   627.12 ÷ 2.01 = _____

239.61 ÷ 1.63 = _____   146.28 ÷ 5.52 = _____

193.41 ÷ 3.15 = _____   232.22 ÷ 6.83 = _____

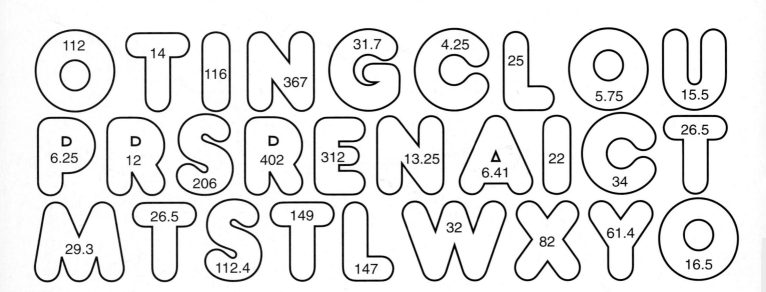

Parent Communication and Student Checkups

Parent Communication and Student Checkups

Table of Contents

How to Administer the Checkups

Both checkups can be given at the same time, or Checkup B can be given as a follow-up test for students who did not do well on Checkup A. The checkups will help you determine which students have mastered a skill and which students need more practice.

Show-Your-Work Grid

For students who need help aligning numbers properly, check out the grid on page 99.

Show Your Work

Name _____ Date _____

Student Progress Chart

_____ (student)		Date	Number Correct	Comments
Checkup 1: Reading and writing mixed decimals	A			
	B			
Checkup 2: Comparing and ordering decimals	A			
	B			
Checkup 3: Adding mixed decimals to thousandths	A			
	B			
Checkup 4: Using equivalent decimals to add mixed decimals to hundredths	A			
	B			
Checkup 5: Using equivalent decimals to add mixed decimals to thousandths	A			
	B			
Checkup 6: Subtracting mixed decimals to thousandths	A			
	B			
Checkup 7: Using equivalent decimals to subtract mixed decimals to hundredths	A			
	B			
Checkup 8: Using equivalent decimals to subtract mixed decimals to thousandths	A			
	B			

Student Progress Chart

_____ (student)		Date	Number Correct	Comments
Checkup 9: Multiplying decimals to hundredths by whole numbers	A			
	B			
Checkup 10: Multiplying decimals to hundredths	A			
	B			
Checkup 11: Multiplying mixed decimals to hundredths	A			
	B			
Checkup 12: Multiplying mixed decimals to thousandths	A			
	B			
Checkup 13: Dividing mixed decimals to thousandths by whole numbers	A			
	B			
Checkup 14: Dividing whole numbers by decimals to hundredths	A			
	B			
Checkup 15: Dividing mixed decimals to hundredths	A			
	B			

It's Time to Take Aim!

On _____ our class will be having a checkup on reading and writing decimals. To help your child prepare, please spend about 20 minutes reviewing math problems that involve **reading and writing mixed decimals.** Thanks for your help!

Decimals Refresher

Need help explaining reading and writing mixed decimals to your child? Try using the two-step method below. Walk your child through the first problem at the right using this method. Next, have him complete the second problem on his own, verbalizing each step as he solves the problem. Then have him complete the remaining problems independently.

Step 1
Read.

56.897

Step 2
Write the decimal in word form.

fifty-six and eight hundred ninety-seven thousandths

OR

Step 1:
Read.
sixty-nine and four tenths

Step 2:
Write the decimal in standard form.

69.4

Try using these two steps!

Target These!

Write each decimal in word form.

56.897	27.43
9.418	226.79
	35.667

Write each decimal in standard form.

sixty-nine and four tenths

nine and thirty six hundredths

twelve and forty-eight hundredths

sixteen and seven hundred fifty-two thousandths

nine hundred two and fifteen thousandths

Answers: fifty-six and eight hundred ninety-seven thousandths, twenty-seven and forty-three hundredths, nine and four hundred eighteen thousandths, two hundred twenty-six and seventy-nine hundredths, thirty-five and six hundred sixty-seven thousandths, 69.4, 9.36, 12.48, 16.752, 902.015

If your child is quick to solve the remaining math problems correctly, an occasional review may be all he needs. But if several of the answers are incorrect, it's a good idea to spend some time each day having your child work through a problem or two at home until he's mastered this skill.

Checkup 1

Name _____ Date _____

Write each decimal in word form.

A.   8.24   17.8

B.   35.412   205.37

Write each decimal in standard form.

C.   seven and nine tenths

D.   fifteen and thirty-five hundredths

E.   sixty-three and sixty-two thousandths

F.   three hundred four and ninety-one hundredths

G.   eighty-four and seven hundredths

H.   five hundred two and one hundred one thousandths

Test A: Reading and writing mixed decimals

©The Education Center, Inc. • *Target Math Success* • TEC60834 • Key p. 143

Checkup 1

Name _____ Date _____

Write each decimal in word form.

A.   6.35   22.4

B.   51.77   108.627

Write each decimal in standard form.

C.   five and six tenths

D.   twenty-seven and thirteen hundredths

E.   eighty-two and thirty-five thousandths

F.   four hundred ninety-three and forty-two hundredths

G.   ninety and two thousandths

H.   three hundred five and seven tenths

Test B: Reading and writing mixed decimals

©The Education Center, Inc. • *Target Math Success* • TEC60834 • Key p. 143

It's Time to Take Aim!

On _____ our class will be having a checkup on comparing and ordering decimals. To help your child prepare, please spend about 20 minutes reviewing math problems that involve **comparing and ordering decimals.** Thanks for your help!

Target These!

Compare the decimals.

4.56 ◯ 4.23

0.7 ◯ 0.97

6.82 ◯ 6.71

12.23 ◯ 12.79

4.06 ◯ 4.061

Order the decimals from least to greatest.

9.62, 9.67, 9.61

0.4, 0.01, 0.06

5.19, 5.21, 5.14

17.31, 17.38, 17.30

3.14, 3.24, 3.21

Decimals Refresher

Need help explaining comparing and ordering decimals to your child? Try using the methods below. Walk your child through the first problem at the right using this method. Next, have him complete the second problem on his own, verbalizing each step as he solves the problem. Then have him complete the remaining problems independently.

Comparing Decimals

Step 1
Line up the numbers by their decimal points.

    4.56
    4.23

Step 2
Starting at the left, compare the digits.

    4.56   4.56
    4.23   4.23
    ↑   ↑
Same number of ones   *5 > 2*
        So, 4.56 > 4.23

Ordering Decimals

Step 1
Line up the numbers by their decimal points.

    9.62
    9.67
    9.61

Step 2
Starting at the left, compare the digits.

    9.62   9.62
    9.67   9.67   *7 > 2*
    9.61   9.61   *2 > 1*
    ↑↑   ↑
Same number of ones and tens

Step 3
Order the numbers from least to greatest.

    9.61, 9.62, 9.67

Try using these steps!

Answers: >; <; >; <; <;
9.61, 9.62, 9.67; 0.01,
0.06, 0.4; 5.14, 5.19, 5.21;
17.30, 17.31, 17.38; 3.14,
3.21, 3.24

If your child is quick to solve the remaining math problems correctly, an occasional review may be all he needs. But if several of the answers are incorrect, it's a good idea to spend some time each day having your child work through a problem or two at home until he's mastered this skill.

Checkup 2

Name _____ Date _____

Compare the decimals.
Write >, <, or =.

A. 0.46 ◯ 0.49

B. 7.326 ◯ 7.356

C. 28.96 ◯ 28.94

Order the decimals from least to greatest.

D. 0.9, 0.89, 0.83 _____

E. 8.04, 8.14, 8.4 _____

2.51 ◯ 2.47

14.05 ◯ 14.5

6.018 ◯ 6.02

2.52, 2.57, 2.5 _____

3.63, 3.61, 3.68 _____

Test A: Comparing and ordering decimals

Checkup 2

Name _____ Date _____

Compare the decimals.
Write >, <, or =.

A. 8.06 ◯ 8.6

B. 14.25 ◯ 14.02

C. 32.04 ◯ 32.014

Order the decimals from least to greatest.

D. 4.1, 4.17, 4.01 _____

E. 6.53, 6.35, 6.5 _____

0.013 ◯ 0.13

1.57 ◯ 1.52

9.62 ◯ 9.68

2.05, 2.55, 2.51 _____

0.82, 0.81, 0.8 _____

Test B: Comparing and ordering decimals

It's Time to Take Aim!

On _____ our class will be having a checkup on adding decimals. To help your child prepare, please spend about 20 minutes reviewing math problems that involve **adding mixed decimals to thousandths.** Thanks for your help!

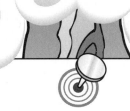

Target These!

$$14.734 + 2.453$$

$$16.42 + 8.90$$

$$\$42.56 + 9.25$$

$$4.568 + 2.149$$

$$14.5 + 8.6 =$$

$$27.12 + 5.39 =$$

$$\$42.85 + \$8.23 =$$

$$20.107 + 8.463 =$$

$$171.45 + 22.34 =$$

$$75.926 + 19.157 =$$

Decimals Refresher

Need help explaining to your child how to add mixed decimals to thousandths? Try using the three-step method below. Walk your child through the first problem at the right using this method. Next, have him complete the second problem on his own, verbalizing each step as he solves the problem. Then have him complete the remaining problems independently.

Try using these three steps!

Step 1
Line up the numbers by their decimal points.

$$14.734 + 2.453$$

Step 2
Add.

$$\begin{array}{r} 14.734 \\ + 2.453 \\ \hline 17\ 187 \end{array}$$

Step 3
Place a decimal point in the answer directly below the decimal points in the problem.

$$\begin{array}{r} 14.734 \\ + 2.453 \\ \hline 17.187 \end{array}$$

Answers: 17.187, 25.32, $51.81, 6.717, 23.1, 32.51, $51.08, 28.57, 193.79, 95.083

If your child is quick to solve the remaining math problems correctly, an occasional review may be all he needs. But if several of the answers are incorrect, it's a good idea to spend some time each day having your child work through a problem or two at home until he's mastered this skill.

Checkup 3

Name _____ Date _____

Add.

A.
```
    23.3        $19.45        7.532        30.47
  + 32.2      + $7.56      + 4.218      + 4.06
```

B.   24.3 + 2.6 = $44.59 + $5.33 =

C.   48.804 + 8.231 =   17.17 + 7.31 =

D.   204.965 + 81.005 = $75.42 + $2.75 =

Test A: Adding mixed decimals to thousandths

Checkup 3

Name _____ Date _____

Add.

A.
```
    4.9        $11.52        45.35        16.409
  + 2.6      + $1.31      + 8.76      + 7.446
```

B.   97.6 + 4.9 = $28.46 + $6.45 =

C.   21.049 + 5.126 =   42.09 + 6.85 =

D.   341.023 + 761.79 = $25.82 + $6.75 =

Test B: Adding mixed decimals to thousandths

It's Time to Take Aim!

On _____ our class will be having a checkup on adding decimals. To help your child prepare, please spend about 20 minutes reviewing math problems that involve **using equivalent decimals to add mixed decimals to hundredths.** Thanks for your help!

Decimals Refresher

Need help explaining to your child how to use equivalent decimals to add mixed decimals to hundredths? Try using the four-step method below. Walk your child through the first problem at the right using this method. Next, have him complete the second problem on his own, verbalizing each step as he solves the problem. Then have him complete the remaining problems independently.

Step 1
Line up the numbers by their decimal points.

$$\begin{array}{r} 2.4 \\ + 1.38 \\ \hline \end{array}$$

Step 2
Write an equivalent decimal so that both numbers have the same number of digits.

$$\begin{array}{r} 2.40 \\ + 1.38 \\ \hline \end{array}$$ ⟵   2.4 = 2.40

Step 3
Do: Add.

$$\begin{array}{r} 2.40 \\ + 1.38 \\ \hline 378 \end{array}$$

Step 4
Place the decimal point in the answer directly below the decimal points in the problem.

$$\begin{array}{r} 2.40 \\ + 1.38 \\ \hline 3.78 \end{array}$$

Try using these four steps!

Target These!

$$\begin{array}{r} 2.4 \\ + 1.38 \\ \hline \end{array} \qquad \begin{array}{r} 17.98 \\ + 5.5 \\ \hline \end{array}$$

$$\begin{array}{r} 4.6 \\ + 1.75 \\ \hline \end{array} \qquad \begin{array}{r} 23.5 \\ + 6.24 \\ \hline \end{array}$$

87.9 + 4.06 =

18.47 + 3.8 =

47.05 + 6.3 =

37.6 + 5.03 =

10.5 + 3.79 =

4.82 + 1.7 =

Answers: 3.78, 23.48, 6.35, 29.74, 91.96, 22.27, 53.35, 42.63, 14.29, 6.52

If your child is quick to solve the remaining math problems correctly, an occasional review may be all he needs. But if several of the answers are incorrect, it's a good idea to spend some time each day having your child work through a problem or two at home until he's mastered this skill.

Checkup 4

Name _____   Date _____

Add.

A.   7.45   10.6   9.82   28.7
   + 2.8   + 2.45   + 1.4   + 3.78

B. 35.05 + 17.2 =   6.7 + 3.59 =

C. 50.75 + 8.5 =   74.6 + 3.84 =

D. 36.9 + 5.09 =   142.25 + 30.7 =

Checkup 4

Name _____   Date _____

Add.

A.   5.75   20.8   16.36   39.1
   + 3.4   + 3.59   + 4.2   + 4.67

B. 42.18 + 12.8 =   9.8 + 6.43 =

C. 24.24 + 6.8 =   13.5 + 4.72 =

D. 58.4 + 3.06 =   206.48 + 25.5 =

It's Time to Take Aim!

On _____ our class will be having a checkup on adding decimals. To help your child prepare, please spend about 20 minutes reviewing math problems that involve **using equivalent decimals to add mixed decimals to thousandths.** Thanks for your help!

Adding Decimals Refresher

Need help explaining to your child how to use equivalent decimals to add mixed decimals to thousandths? Try using the four-step method below. Walk your child through the first problem at the right using this method. Next, have him complete the second problem on his own, verbalizing each step as he solves the problem. Then have him complete the remaining problems independently.

Step 1
Line up the numbers by their decimal points.

```
  14.567
+  7.3
```

Step 2
Write an equivalent decimal so that both numbers have the same number of digits.

```
  14.567
+  7.300  ◀——  7.3 = 7.300
```

Step 3
Add.

```
  14.567
+  7.300
  21867
```

Step 4
Place the decimal point in the answer directly below the decimal points in the problem.

```
  14.567
+  7.300
  21.867
        ↑
```

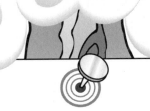

Target These!

```
  14.567          5.82
+  7.3         + 3.479
```

```
  22.5          48.561
+  8.436       +  4.4
```

26.571 + 10.3 =

60.3 + 8.543 =

9.75 + 3.025 =

85.305 + 9.25 =

13.4 + 7.015 =

35.075 + 4.8 =

Try using these four steps!

Answers: 21.867, 9.299, 30.936, 52.961, 36.871, 68.843, 12.775, 94.555, 20.415, 39.875

If your child is quick to solve the remaining math problems correctly, an occasional review may be all he needs. But if several of the answers are incorrect, it's a good idea to spend some time each day having your child work through a problem or two at home until he's mastered this skill.

Checkup 5

Name _____ Date _____

Add.

A. $\begin{array}{r} 13.546 \\ +\ 8.25 \\ \hline \end{array}$ $\begin{array}{r} 9.75 \\ +\ 3.4 \\ \hline \end{array}$ $\begin{array}{r} 37.42 \\ +\ 6.208 \\ \hline \end{array}$ $\begin{array}{r} 206.3 \\ +\ 81.1 \\ \hline \end{array}$

B. 25.406 + 7.5 =   6.3 + 1.228 =

C. 210.9 + 48.245 =   8.702 + 7.8 =

D. 53.42 + 5.5 =   178.6 + 43.219 =

Checkup 5

Name _____ Date _____

Add.

A. $\begin{array}{r} 6.38 \\ +\ 4.2 \\ \hline \end{array}$ $\begin{array}{r} 10.8 \\ +\ 6.584 \\ \hline \end{array}$ $\begin{array}{r} 22.56 \\ +\ 7.105 \\ \hline \end{array}$ $\begin{array}{r} 540.5 \\ +\ 62.59 \\ \hline \end{array}$

B. 36.652 + 8.8 =   8.4 + 2.068 =

C. 100.5 + 25.075 =   9.684 + 3.7 =

D. 49.17 + 8.7 =   346.1 + 50.334 =

It's Time to Take Aim!

On _____ our class will be having a checkup on subtracting decimals. To help your child prepare, please spend about 20 minutes reviewing math problems that involve **subtracting mixed decimals to thousandths.** Thanks for your help!

Target These!

$$25.56 - 7.24$$

$$67.45 - 9.38$$

$$63.562 - 8.417$$

$$108.46 - 42.71$$

$$93.42 - 13.76 =$$

$$9.24 - 6.69 =$$

$$88.95 - 13.23 =$$

$$415.5 - 76.3 =$$

$$13.274 - 2.681 =$$

$$\$34.56 - \$5.25 =$$

Decimals Refresher

Need help explaining to your child how to subtract mixed decimals to thousandths? Try using the three-step method below. Walk your child through the first problem at the right using this method. Next, have him complete the second problem on his own, verbalizing each step as he solves the problem. Then have him complete the remaining problems independently.

Try using these three steps!

Step 1
Line up the numbers by their decimal points.

$$25.56 - 7.24$$

Step 2
Subtract.

$$\overset{1}{\cancel{2}}5.56 - 7.24 = 18.32$$

Step 3
Place the decimal point in the answer directly below the decimal points in the problem.

$$25.56 - 7.24 = 18.32$$

If your child is quick to solve the remaining math problems correctly, an occasional review may be all he needs. But if several of the answers are incorrect, it's a good idea to spend some time each day having your child work through a problem or two at home until he's mastered this skill.

Checkup 6

Name _____ Date _____

Subtract.

A.   50.5   \$74.92   256.2   17.436
   − 12.3   − 7.67   − 17.5   − 2.311

B.   24.7 − 8.2 =

C.   84.73 − 12.45 =

      145.2 − 83.7 =

D.   4.678 − 2.453 =

      22.567 − 8.431 =

Test A: Subtracting mixed decimals to thousandths

©The Education Center, Inc. • *Target Math Success* • TEC60834 • Key p. 143

Checkup 6

Name _____ Date _____

Subtract.

A.   25.1   \$9.74   65.72   17.436
   − 16.4   − \$5.05   − 8.59   − 4.321

B.   \$34.78 − \$12.93 =

      59.456 − 6.384 =

C.   505.6 − 82.8 =

      75.43 − 4.88 =

D.   12.456 − 3.218 =

      207.8 − 5.4 =

Test B: Subtracting mixed decimals to thousandths

©The Education Center, Inc. • *Target Math Success* • TEC60834 • Key p. 143

It's Time to Take Aim!

On _____ our class will be having a checkup on subtracting decimals. To help your child prepare, please spend about 20 minutes reviewing math problems that involve **using equivalent decimals to subtract mixed decimals to hundredths.** Thanks for your help!

Target These!

$$
\begin{array}{r} 4.3 \\ -\ 2.15 \\ \hline \end{array}
\qquad
\begin{array}{r} 8.7 \\ -\ 4.25 \\ \hline \end{array}
$$

$$
\begin{array}{r} 12.53 \\ -\ 9.2 \\ \hline \end{array}
\qquad
\begin{array}{r} 22.6 \\ -\ 8.59 \\ \hline \end{array}
$$

$34.8 - 16.26 =$

$9.43 - 2.1 =$

$15.68 - 0.5 =$

$75.4 - 50.27 =$

$61.32 - 40.5 =$

$17.4 - 8.35 =$

Decimals Refresher

Need help explaining to your child how to use equivalent decimals to subtract mixed decimals to hundredths? Try using the four-step method below. Walk your child through the first problem at the right using this method. Next, have him complete the second problem on his own, verbalizing each step as he solves the problem. Then have him complete the remaining problems independently.

Step 1
Line up the numbers by their decimal points.

$$
\begin{array}{r} 4.3 \\ -\ 2.15 \\ \hline \end{array}
$$

Step 2
Write an equivalent decimal so that both numbers have the same number of digits.

$$
\begin{array}{r} 4.3\mathbf{0} \\ -\ 2.15 \\ \hline \end{array}
\quad \longleftarrow \ 4.3 = 4.30
$$

Step 3
Subtract.

$$
\begin{array}{r} 4.\overset{2\ 1}{\cancel{3}}0 \\ -\ 2.15 \\ \hline 2\ 15 \end{array}
$$

Step 4
Place the decimal point in the answer directly below the decimal points in the problem.

$$
\begin{array}{r} 4.30 \\ -\ 2.15 \\ \hline 2.15 \end{array}
$$

<speech bubble> Try using these four steps!

If your child is quick to solve the remaining math problems correctly, an occasional review may be all he needs. But if several of the answers are incorrect, it's a good idea to spend some time each day having your child work through a problem or two at home until he's mastered this skill.

Checkup 7

Name _____ Date _____

Subtract.

A.
$$9.8$$
$$-\ 6.34$$

$$7.54$$
$$-\ 2.1$$

$$15.8$$
$$-\ 7.62$$

$$28.25$$
$$-\ 5.5$$

B. $12.5 - 10.75 =$

C. $36.8 - 0.75 =$

D. $88.4 - 7.82$

Test A: Using equivalent decimals to subtract mixed decimals to hundredths

©The Education Center, Inc. • *Target Math Success* • TEC60834 • Key p. 143

Checkup 7

Name _____ Date _____

Subtract.

A.
$$5.68$$
$$-\ 3.2$$

$$4.9$$
$$-\ 2.07$$

$$10.3$$
$$-\ 2.57$$

$$9.82$$
$$-\ 5.5$$

B. $13.31 - 5.8 =$

$24.5 - 17.39 =$

C. $21.48 - 7.8 =$

$61.3 - 20.04 =$

D. $50.7 - 25.25 =$

$81.95 - 7.2 =$

Test B: Using equivalent decimals to subtract mixed decimals to hundredths

©The Education Center, Inc. • *Target Math Success* • TEC60834 • Key p. 143

It's Time to Take Aim!

On _____ our class will be having a checkup on subtracting decimals. To help your child prepare, please spend about 20 minutes reviewing math problems that involve **using equivalent decimals to subtract mixed decimals to thousandths.** Thanks for your help!

Decimals Refresher

Need help explaining to your child how to use equivalent decimals to subtract mixed decimals to thousandths? Try using the four-step method below. Walk your child through the first problem at the right using this method. Next, have him complete the second problem on his own, verbalizing each step as he solves the problem. Then have him complete the remaining problems independently.

Step 1
Line up the numbers by their decimal points.

$$\begin{array}{r} 21.465 \\ -\ 8.3 \\ \hline \end{array}$$

Step 2
Write an equivalent decimal so that both numbers have the same number of digits.

$$\begin{array}{r} 21.465 \\ -\ 8.3\mathbf{00} \\ \hline \end{array}$$ ⬅ 8.3 = 8.300

Step 3
Subtract.

$$\begin{array}{r} 21.465 \\ -\ 8.300 \\ \hline 13\ 165 \end{array}$$

Step 4
Place the decimal point in the answer directly below the decimal points in the problem.

$$\begin{array}{r} 21.465 \\ -\ 8.300 \\ \hline 13.165 \end{array}$$
⬆

Try using these four steps!

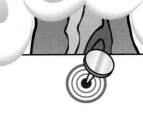

Target These!

$$\begin{array}{r} 21.465 \\ -\ 8.3 \\ \hline \end{array} \qquad \begin{array}{r} 12.916 \\ -\ 2.5 \\ \hline \end{array}$$

$$\begin{array}{r} 9.7 \\ -\ 5.351 \\ \hline \end{array} \qquad \begin{array}{r} 24.682 \\ -\ 4.6 \\ \hline \end{array}$$

$57.4 - 5.042 =$

$18.321 - 10.76 =$

$26.5 - 4.318 =$

$44.561 - 20.5 =$

$68.4 - 9.615 =$

$28.765 - 5.7 =$

Answers: 13.165, 10.416, 4.349, 20.082, 52.358, 7.561, 22.182, 24.061, 58.785, 23.065

If your child is quick to solve the remaining math problems correctly, an occasional review may be all he needs. But if several of the answers are incorrect, it's a good idea to spend some time each day having your child work through a problem or two at home until he's mastered this skill.

Checkup 8

Name _____ Date _____

Subtract.

A.
16.568
− 4.32

9.8
− 1.684

7.48
− 5.269

26.7
− 8.148

B. 34.752 − 20.53 =

9.456 − 2.8 =

C. 18.9 − 6.432 =

56.812 − 7.4 =

D. 38.6 − 5.319 =

85.415 − 3.8 =

Test A: Using equivalent decimals to subtract mixed decimals to thousandths

©The Education Center, Inc. • *Target Math Success* • TEC60834 • Key p. 143

Checkup 8

Name _____ Date _____

Subtract.

A.
15.217
− 8.34

9.3
− 2.561

6.54
− 1.893

31.5
− 10.216

B. 43.801 − 20.7 =

8.744 − 3.8 =

C. 36.7 − 9.246 =

75.284 − 5.9 =

D. 41.3 − 10.468 =

62.507 − 7.4 =

Test B: Using equivalent decimals to subtract mixed decimals to thousandths

©The Education Center, Inc. • *Target Math Success* • TEC60834 • Key p. 143

It's Time to Take Aim!

On _____ our class will be having a checkup on multiplying decimals. To help your child prepare, please spend about 20 minutes reviewing math problems that involve **multiplying decimals to hundredths by whole numbers.** Thanks for your help!

Decimals Refresher

Need help explaining to your child how to multiply decimals to hundredths by whole numbers? Try using the three-step method below. Walk your child through the first problem at the right using this method. Next, have him complete the second problem on his own, verbalizing each step as he solves the problem. Then have him complete the remaining problems independently.

Step 1
Multiply.

$$
\begin{array}{r} 0.3 \\ \times\ 5 \\ \hline 15 \end{array}
\qquad
\begin{array}{r} 0.16 \\ \times\ 6 \\ \hline 96 \end{array}
$$

Step 2
Count the number of places to the right of the decimal.

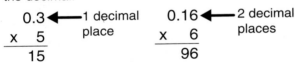

$$
\begin{array}{r} 0.3 \\ \times\ 5 \\ \hline 15 \end{array}
$$
←— 1 decimal place

$$
\begin{array}{r} 0.16 \\ \times\ 6 \\ \hline 96 \end{array}
$$
←— 2 decimal places

Step 3
Start at the right side of the answer and count over the same number of places. Place the decimal point.

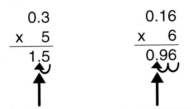

$$
\begin{array}{r} 0.3 \\ \times\ 5 \\ \hline 1.5 \end{array}
\qquad
\begin{array}{r} 0.16 \\ \times\ 6 \\ \hline 0.96 \end{array}
$$

Try using these three steps!

Target These!

$$
\begin{array}{r} 0.3 \\ \times\ 5 \\ \hline \end{array}
\qquad
\begin{array}{r} 0.9 \\ \times\ 7 \\ \hline \end{array}
$$

$$
\begin{array}{r} 0.8 \\ \times\ 8 \\ \hline \end{array}
\qquad
\begin{array}{r} 0.37 \\ \times\ 5 \\ \hline \end{array}
$$

$$
\begin{array}{r} 0.01 \\ \times\ 6 \\ \hline \end{array}
\qquad
\begin{array}{r} 0.19 \\ \times\ 6 \\ \hline \end{array}
$$

0.12 x 4 =

54 x 0.8 =

23 x 0.14 =

0.46 x 81 =

Answers: 1.5, 6.3, 6.4, 1.85, 0.06, 1.14, 0.48, 43.2, 3.22, 37.26

If your child is quick to solve the remaining math problems correctly, an occasional review may be all he needs. But if several of the answers are incorrect, it's a good idea to spend some time each day having your child work through a problem or two at home until he's mastered this skill.

Checkup 9

Multiply.

A. 0.41   0.13   36
    x   3   x 42   x 0.8

B. 19   0.73
    x 0.6   x 34

C. 0.8 x 9 =

D. 0.47 x 5 =   54 x 0.3 =

Test A: Multiplying decimals to hundredths by whole numbers

©The Education Center, Inc. • *Target Math Success* • TEC60834 • Key p. 143

Checkup 9

Multiply.

A. 0.5   0.39   78
    x   6   x   9   x 0.6

B. 0.24   71   0.15
    x 42   x 0.8   x 63

C. 0.69 x 6 =   55 x 0.5 =

D. 169 x 0.4 =   0.17 x 26 =

Test B: Multiplying decimals to hundredths by whole numbers

©The Education Center, Inc. • *Target Math Success* • TEC60834 • Key p. 143

It's Time to Take Aim!

On _____ our class will be having a checkup on multiplying decimals. To help your child prepare, please spend about 20 minutes reviewing math problems that involve **multiplying decimals to hundredths.** Thanks for your help!

Target These!

$$0.15 \times 0.3$$

$$0.3 \times 0.7$$

$$0.14 \times 0.2$$

$$0.38 \times 0.4$$

$$0.62 \times 0.5$$

$$0.21 \times 0.93$$

$$0.47 \times 0.81 =$$

$$0.53 \times 0.17 =$$

$$0.72 \times 0.93 =$$

$$0.46 \times 0.31 =$$

Decimals Refresher

Need help explaining to your child how to multiply decimals to hundredths? Try using the three-step method below. Walk your child through the first problem at the right using this method. Next, have him complete the second problem on his own, verbalizing each step as he solves the problem. Then have him complete the remaining problems independently.

Try using these three steps!

Step 1
Multiply.

$$0.15 \times 0.3 = 045$$

Step 2
Count the number of places to the right of the decimal.

0.15 ⟵ 2 decimal places
x 0.3 ⟵ 1 decimal place
045   3 total places

Step 3
Starting at the right side of the answer, count over the same number of places. Place the decimal point.

$$0.15 \times 0.3 = 0.045$$

Answers: 0.045, 0.21, 0.028, 0.152, 0.310, 0.1953, 0.3807, 0.0901, 0.6696, 0.1426

If your child is quick to solve the remaining math problems correctly, an occasional review may be all he needs. But if several of the answers are incorrect, it's a good idea to spend some time each day having your child work through a problem or two at home until he's mastered this skill.

Checkup 10

Name _____

Date _____

Multiply.

A.   0.3   0.27   0.41
  x 0.4   x 0.5   x 0.8

B.   0.16   0.39   0.75
  x 0.24   x 0.7   x 0.33

C. 0.7 x 0.4 =   0.9 x 0.3 =

D. 0.96 x 0.4 =   0.49 x 0.58 =

Checkup 10

Name _____

Date _____

Multiply.

A.   0.6   0.4   0.34   0.62
  x 0.7   x 0.9   x 0.2   x 0.7

B.   0.46   0.27   0.52   0.76
  x 0.26   x 0.38   x 0.3   x 0.19

C. 0.8 x 0.5 =   0.2 x 0.8 =

D. 0.3 x 0.74 =   0.85 x 0.29 =

It's Time to Take Aim!

On _____ our class will be having a checkup on multiplying decimals. To help your child prepare, please spend about 20 minutes reviewing math problems that involve **multiplying mixed decimals to hundredths by a whole number.** Thanks for your help!

Decimals Refresher

Need help explaining to your child how to multiply mixed decimals to hundredths by a whole number? Try using the three-step method below. Walk your child through the first problem at the right using this method. Next, have him complete the second problem on his own, verbalizing each step as he solves the problem. Then have him complete the remaining problems independently.

Step 1
Multiply.

$$\begin{array}{r} 3.9 \\ \times\ 2 \\ \hline 7\,8 \end{array}$$

Step 2
Count the number of places to the right of the decimal.

$$\begin{array}{r} 3.9 \\ \times\ 2 \\ \hline 7\,8 \end{array}$$
3.9 ⟵ 1 decimal place
x 2 ⟵ 0 decimal places
7 8   1 total place

Step 3
Starting at the right side of the answer, count over the number of places. Place the decimal point.

$$\begin{array}{r} 3.9 \\ \times\ 2 \\ \hline 7.8 \end{array}$$

Try using these three steps!

Target These!

$$\begin{array}{r} 3.9 \\ \times\ 2 \\ \hline \end{array} \qquad \begin{array}{r} 18.6 \\ \times\ 7 \\ \hline \end{array}$$

$$\begin{array}{r} 2.31 \\ \times\ 5 \\ \hline \end{array} \qquad \begin{array}{r} 8.96 \\ \times\ 2 \\ \hline \end{array}$$

$$\begin{array}{r} 7.5 \\ \times\ 9 \\ \hline \end{array} \qquad \begin{array}{r} 6.25 \\ \times\ 4 \\ \hline \end{array}$$

$19.2 \times 8 =$

$1.76 \times 6 =$

$7.53 \times 6 =$

$9.35 \times 3 =$

Answers: 7.8, 130.2, 11.55, 17.92, 67.5, 25, 153.6, 10.56, 45.18, 28.05

If your child is quick to solve the remaining math problems correctly, an occasional review may be all he needs. But if several of the answers are incorrect, it's a good idea to spend some time each day having your child work through a problem or two at home until he's mastered this skill.

Checkup 11

Name _____

Date _____

Multiply.

A.   2.5   3.5   4.83   5.06
   x 8   x 9   x 4   x 3

B.   11.8   2.39   9.2   16.4
   x 7   x 6   x 5   x 2

C. 7.4 x 3 =   19.36 x 5 =

D. 6.4 x 8 =   9.06 x 4 =

Test A: Multiplying mixed decimals to hundredths by whole numbers

©The Education Center, Inc. • *Target Math Success* • TEC60834 • Key p. 143

123

Checkup 11

Name _____

Date _____

Multiply.

A.   12.8   3.64   2.4   8.6
   x 9   x 7   x 5   x 4

B.   9.72   7.41   5.3   11.9
   x 3   x 2   x 8   x 6

C. 13.6 x 4 =   7.63 x 3 =

D. 5.42 x 6 =   9.4 x 9 =

Test B: Multiplying mixed decimals to hundredths by whole numbers

©The Education Center, Inc. • *Target Math Success* • TEC60834 • Key p. 143

It's Time to Take Aim!

On _____ our class will be having a checkup on multiplying decimals. To help your child prepare, please spend about 20 minutes reviewing math problems that involve **multiplying mixed decimals to thousandths.** Thanks for your help!

Target These!

2.312 x 1.05	3.15 x 2.6
4.38 x 4.9	2.88 x 6.5
1.172 x 3.42	5.341 x 2.73

Try using these three steps!

Decimals Refresher

Need help explaining multiplying mixed decimals to thousandths to your child? Try using the three-step method below. Walk your child through the first problem at the right using this method. Next, have him complete the second problem on his own, verbalizing each step as he solves the problem. Then have him complete the remaining problems independently.

Step 1
Multiply.

```
    2.312
  x 1.05
    11560
    00000
+ 231200
  242760
```

Step 2
Count the number of places to the right of each decimal.

```
    2.312  ←  3 decimal places
  x 1.05   ←  2 decimal places
    11560      5 total places
    00000
+ 231200
  242760
```

Step 3
Starting at the right side of the answer, count over the same number of places. Place the decimal point.

2.42760

1.12 x 3.4 =

4.17 x 1.24 =

2.53 x 3.86 =

9.42 x 7.35 =

Answers: 2.42760, 8.19, 21.462, 18.72, 4.00824, 14.58093, 3.808, 5.1708, 9.7658, 69.2370

If your child is quick to solve the remaining math problems correctly, an occasional review may be all he needs. But if several of the answers are incorrect, it's a good idea to spend some time each day having your child work through a problem or two at home until he's mastered this skill.

Checkup 12

Name _____

Date _____

Multiply.

A.
```
   2.8        3.1        2.53        7.42
 x 5.3      x 4.9      x 1.7       x 3.2
```

B.
```
   4.82                  5.38        3.795
 x 6.25                x 2.89      x 2.26
```

C. $14.4 \times 9.6 =$ $9.7 \times 3.2 =$ $4.12 \times 3.62 =$

Test A: Multiplying mixed decimals to thousandths

Checkup 12

Name _____

Date _____

Multiply.

A.
```
   6.5        7.2        6.97        17.5
 x 2.3      x 4.5      x 3.5       x 3.4
```

B.
```
   6.33                 3.59        4.342
 x 4.56              x 2.67      x 1.58
```

C. $5.7 \times 1.6 =$ $6.543 \times 8.69 =$ $4.21 \times 6.83 =$

Test B: Multiplying mixed decimals to thousandths

It's Time to Take Aim!

On _____ our class will be having a checkup on dividing mixed decimals. To help your child prepare, please spend about 20 minutes reviewing math problems that involve **dividing mixed decimals to thousandths by a whole number.** Thanks for your help!

Target These!

$$6\overline{)21.84} \qquad 6\overline{)15.18}$$

$$4\overline{)24.68} \qquad 5\overline{)498.5}$$

Try using these two steps!

$$9\overline{)794.61} \qquad 7\overline{)1.694}$$

Decimals Refresher

Need help explaining to your child how to divide mixed decimals to thousandths by a whole number? Try using the two-step method below. Walk your child through the first problem at the right using this method. Next, have him complete the second problem on his own, verbalizing each step as he solves the problem. Then have him complete the remaining problems independently.

Step 1
Place the decimal point in the answer directly above the decimal point in the problem.

$$6\overline{)21.84}$$

Step 2
Divide.

$$\begin{array}{r} 3.64 \\ 6\overline{)21.84} \\ -\ 18 \\ \hline 38 \\ -\ 36 \\ \hline 24 \\ -\ 24 \\ \hline 0 \end{array}$$

$$15.18 \div 6 =$$

$$42.039 \div 3 =$$

$$98.6 \div 2 =$$

$$21.84 \div 3 =$$

Answers: 3.64, 2.53, 6.17, 99.7, 88.29, 0.242, 2.53, 14.013, 49.3, 7.28

If your child is quick to solve the remaining math problems correctly, an occasional review may be all he needs. But if several of the answers are incorrect, it's a good idea to spend some time each day having your child work through a problem or two at home until he's mastered this skill.

Checkup 13

Name _____ Date _____

Divide.

A. $6\overline{)4.14}$ $3\overline{)1.05}$ $4\overline{)28.8}$ $6\overline{)14.4}$

B. $7\overline{)5.593}$ $4\overline{)1.08}$ $6\overline{)1.98}$ $3\overline{)21.3}$

C. $19.188 \div 6 =$ $1.696 \div 8 =$

D. $59.4 \div 9 =$ $49.12 \div 8 =$

Checkup 13

Name _____ Date _____

Divide.

A. $4\overline{)4.56}$ $7\overline{)3.01}$ $8\overline{)24.8}$ $5\overline{)6.85}$

B. $3\overline{)20.4}$ $9\overline{)3.114}$ $9\overline{)8.739}$ $2\overline{)10.6}$

C. $11.032 \div 8 =$ $6.85 \div 5 =$

D. $48.736 \div 8 =$ $19.188 \div 6 =$

It's Time to Take Aim!

On _____ our class will be having a checkup on dividing with decimals. To help your child prepare, please spend about 20 minutes reviewing math problems that involve **dividing a whole number by a decimal to hundredths.** Thanks for your help!

Decimals Refresher

Need help explaining to your child dividing a whole number by a decimal to hundredths? Try using the three-step method below. Walk your child through the first problem at the right using this method. Next, have him complete the second problem on his own, verbalizing each step as he solves the problem. Then have him complete the remaining problems independently.

Step 1
Make the divisor a whole number by multiplying it and the dividend by a multiple of ten. Move both decimal points to the right the same number of places.

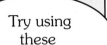

$$0.36 \times 100 = 36$$
$$18 \times 100 = 1800$$

Step 2
Place the decimal point in the quotient directly above the decimal point in the dividend.

$$36. \overline{)1800.}$$

Step 3
Divide. If the answer is a whole number, the decimal point is not needed.

$$
\begin{array}{r}
50 \\
36. \overline{)1800} \\
180 \\
\hline
00 \\
-\ 00 \\
\hline
0
\end{array}
$$

Target These!

$$0.3 \overline{)18} \qquad 0.4 \overline{)32}$$

$$0.9 \overline{)54} \qquad 0.05 \overline{)35}$$

$$0.19 \overline{)76} \qquad 0.8 \overline{)72}$$

$$147 \div 0.21 =$$

$$125 \div 0.05 =$$

$$364 \div 0.7 =$$

$$38 \div 0.2 =$$

Try using these three steps!

Answers: 50, 80, 60, 700, 400, 90, 700, 2500, 520, 190

If your child is quick to solve the remaining math problems correctly, an occasional review may be all he needs. But if several of the answers are incorrect, it's a good idea to spend some time each day having your child work through a problem or two at home until he's mastered this skill.

Checkup 14

Name _____   Date _____

Divide.

A. $0.15 \overline{)30}$ $\$0.22 \overline{)66}$

B. $0.6 \overline{)12}$ $0.07 \overline{)14}$

C. $0.12 \overline{)6}$ $\$0.08 \overline{)4}$

D. $54 \div 0.06 =$ $26 \div \$0.13 =$

Checkup 14

Name _____   Date _____

Divide.

A. $0.4 \overline{)12}$ $0.55 \overline{)22}$ $0.6 \overline{)24}$

B. $\$0.03 \overline{)15}$ $0.14 \overline{)28}$ $0.9 \overline{)45}$

C. $0.8 \overline{)24}$ $\$0.36 \overline{)72}$ $\$0.16 \overline{)8}$

D. $91 \div 0.7 =$ $56 \div 0.28 =$ $92 \div 0.23 =$

It's Time to Take Aim!

On _____ our class will be having a checkup on dividing decimals. To help your child prepare, please spend about 20 minutes reviewing math problems that involve **dividing mixed decimals to hundredths.** Thanks for your help!

Decimals Refresher

Need help explaining to your child dividing mixed decimals to hundredths? Try using the three-step method below. Walk your child through the first problem at the right using this method. Next, have him complete the second problem on his own, verbalizing each step as he solves the problem. Then have him complete the remaining problems independently.

Step 1
Make the divisor a whole number by multiplying it and the dividend by a multiple of ten. Move both decimal points to the right the same number of places.

$$2.36 \overline{)33.04}$$

2.36 x 100 = 236

33.04 x 100 = 3304

Step 2
Place the decimal point in the quotient directly above the decimal point in the dividend.

$$236. \overline{)3304.}$$

Step 3
Divide.

```
        14.
236.) 3304.
    - 236
       944
    -  944
         0
```

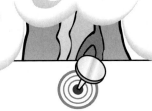

Target These!

$$2.36 \overline{)33.04}$$

$$1.9 \overline{)9.5}$$

$$3.7 \overline{)14.8}$$

$$10.4 \overline{)31.2}$$

$$6.3 \overline{)50.4}$$

$$5.2 \overline{)46.8}$$

$$4.26 \overline{)10.65}$$

$$7.24 \overline{)23.53}$$

$$8.55 \overline{)18.81}$$

$$3.68 \overline{)49.68}$$

Try using these three steps!

Answers: 14, 5, 4, 3, 8, 9, 2.5, 3.25, 2.2, 13.5

If your child is quick to solve the remaining math problems correctly, an occasional review may be all he needs. But if several of the answers are incorrect, it's a good idea to spend some time each day having your child work through a problem or two at home until he's mastered this skill.

Checkup 15

Name _____ Date _____

Divide.

A. 2.4) 8.4   3.2) 19.2   6.5) 7.8

B. 4.05) 25.11   1.63) 70.09

C. 5.12) 43.52   2.38) 22.61

Test A: Dividing mixed decimals to hundredths

©The Education Center, Inc. • Target Math Success • TEC60834 • Key p. 143

Checkup 15

Name _____ Date _____

Divide.

A. 7.1) 35.5   5.2) 49.4   1.6) 19.2

B. 2.43) 53.46   3.72) 24.18

C. 4.16) 13.52   8.35) 70.14

Test B: Dividing mixed decimals to hundredths

©The Education Center, Inc. • Target Math Success • TEC60834 • Key p. 143

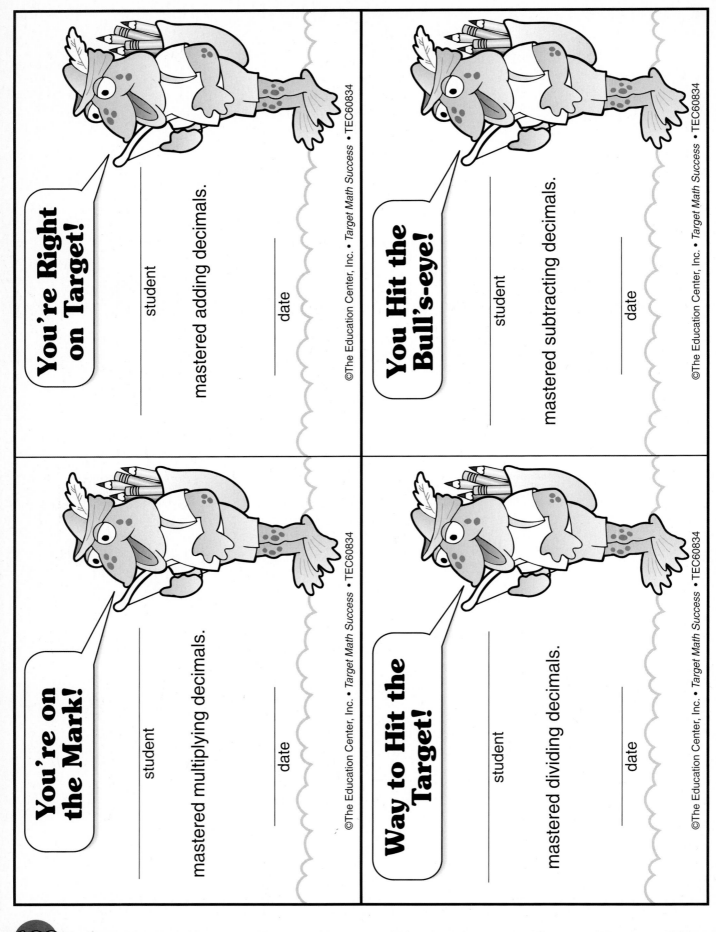

You're Right on Target!

_____
student

mastered adding decimals.

_____
date

You Hit the Bull's-eye!

_____
student

mastered subtracting decimals.

_____
date

You're on the Mark!

_____
student

mastered multiplying decimals.

_____
date

Way to Hit the Target!

_____
student

mastered dividing decimals.

_____
date

Answer Keys

Picnic Lunch

Name _____ Date _____

Write the decimal for the shaded part of each model.
The first one has been done for you.

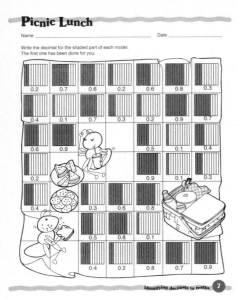

0.2	0.7	0.6	0.2	0.6	0.8	0.3
0.4	0.1	0.7	0.3	0.2	0.9	0.7
0.6	0.9			0.5	0.1	0.4
0.2				0.9		0.3
	0.3	0.6	0.8			
		0.5	0.8	0.1		
0.4	0.8	0.4	0.3	0.8	0.7	0.9

Star Light, Star Bright

Name _____ Date _____

Identify the place of the underlined digit.
Color by the code.

Code
ones or tens = blue
tenths = yellow
hundredths = red
thousandths = green

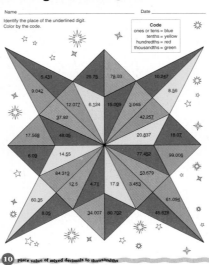

5.431 25.75 78.03 10.247

9.042 8.56

12.077 6.124 15.009 3.045

37.92 42.257

17.568 48.05 20.837 18.07

6.09 14.55 77.452 99.006

84.313 53.679

12.5 4.71 17.9 3.453

60.35 61.094

8.05 34.007 80.702 45.678

Got Jelly?

Name _____ Date _____

Read the written form of each decimal.
Write the decimal in standard form.
Cross off the answer on the coral.

two and eight tenths — 2.8

seventy-eight and two hundredths — 78.02

eighty-four and four hundredths — 84.04

ten and thirteen thousandths — 10.013

five and three thousandths — 5.003

seventy-eight and two tenths — 78.2

one and twelve thousandths — 1.012

one hundred twenty-five and one tenth — 125.1

forty-five and sixteen hundredths — 45.16

fifteen and sixty-seven hundredths — 15.67

thirty-three and eight hundredths — 33.08

six and three hundred twenty-five thousandths — 6.325

6.325 78.2 33.08 45.16
10.013 78.02 1.012
125.1 5.003 84.04 96.5
1.25 2.8 15.67

Slam Dunk!

Name _____ Date _____

Write the decimal for the shaded part of each model.
Cross out the matching answer on the pole.

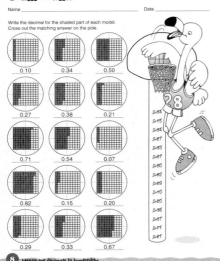

0.10	0.34	0.50
0.27	0.38	0.21
0.71	0.54	0.07
0.82	0.15	0.20
0.29	0.33	0.67

0.54
0.15
0.34
0.27
0.33
0.07
0.50
0.02
0.95
0.10
0.20
0.98
0.67
0.21

And the Winner Is...

Name _____ Date _____

Read the standard form of the decimal.
Color the correct expanded or written form
to show the path to the winner.

On your mark, get set, go!

0.92	0.9 + 0.2	ninety-two hundredths
0.12	twelve hundredths	0.1 + 0.2
0.35	thirty-five hundreds	0.3 + 0.05
0.46	0.4 + 0.06	four tenths
0.5	five tenths	five hundredths
0.72	seventy-two hundreds	seventy-two hundredths
0.67	sixty-seven	0.6 + 0.07
0.28	0.2 + 0.08	twenty-eight tenths
0.19	0.01 + 0.9	nineteen hundredths
0.22	two tenths	0.2 + 0.02
0.7	seven hundredths	seven tenths
0.86	eighty-six hundredths	0.08 + 0.06
0.24	twenty-four tenths	0.2 + 0.04
0.53	0.5 + 0.03	fifty-three hundreds

hummingbird   hawk

No Place Like Home!

Name _____ Date _____

Color if correct.
Connect the colored boxes to draw a path to the magic lamp.

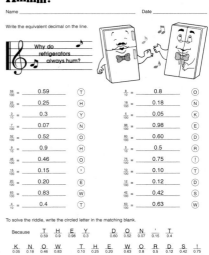

Start

$0.5 = \frac{5}{10}$ $0.29 = \frac{29}{100}$

$0.35 = \frac{35}{100}$

0.03

$0.5 = \frac{5}{10}$

0.60

$0.16 = \frac{16}{100}$ Finish

$0.08 = \frac{8}{100}$

$0.75 = \frac{75}{100}$ $0.44 = \frac{44}{100}$

$0.9 = \frac{9}{10}$

$0.2 = \frac{2}{100}$ $0.44 = \frac{44}{100}$

0.05 $0.9 = \frac{9}{100}$

Magic Show

Name _____ Date _____

Circle the digit in the place noted in parentheses.
Write the circled digit in the magic square below.
The sum of each row and column should equal 20.

1. 0.04 (tenths)
2. 0.789 (thousandths)
3. 0.38 (hundredths)
4. 0.054 (thousandths)
5. 0.881 (tenths)
6. 0.305 (hundredths)
7. 0.75 (tenths)
8. 0.043 (thousandths)
9. 0.267 (hundredths)
10. 0.651 (thousandths)
11. 0.57 (hundredths)
12. 0.805 (tenths)
13. 0.018 (hundredths)
14. 0.92 (tenths)
15. 0.037 (hundredths)
16. 0.593 (tenths)

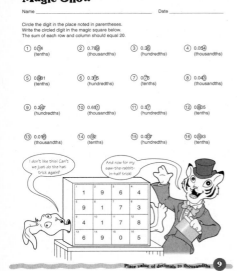

I don't like this! Can't we just do the hat trick again!?

And now for my saw-the-rabbit-in-half trick!

1	9	6	4
9	1	7	3
4	1	7	8
6	9	0	5

Kite Release

Name _____ Date _____

Read each decimal in written and standard form.
Find each matching kite and T-shirt. Color each pair a different color.

eleven thousandths

fifteen hundredths

five thousandths

fifty-three thousandths

sixty-two hundredths

one tenth

eight tenths

seven tenths

four thousandths

twenty-two hundredths

three hundred twenty-one thousandths

0.1 0.053 0.004 0.15 0.321
0.62 0.011 0.7 0.005 0.8

Hmmm?

Name _____ Date _____

Write the equivalent decimal on the line.

Why do refrigerators always hum?

$\frac{59}{100}$ = 0.59 (T)	$\frac{8}{10}$ = 0.8 (O)
$\frac{25}{100}$ = 0.25 (H)	$\frac{18}{100}$ = 0.18 (N)
$\frac{3}{10}$ = 0.3 (Y)	$\frac{5}{100}$ = 0.05 (K)
$\frac{7}{100}$ = 0.07 (N)	$\frac{98}{100}$ = 0.98 (E)
$\frac{52}{100}$ = 0.52 (O)	$\frac{60}{100}$ = 0.60 (D)
$\frac{9}{10}$ = 0.9 (O)	$\frac{5}{10}$ = 0.5 (R)
$\frac{46}{100}$ = 0.46 (O)	$\frac{75}{100}$ = 0.75 (I)
$\frac{15}{100}$ = 0.15 (')	$\frac{10}{100}$ = 0.10 (T)
$\frac{20}{100}$ = 0.20 (E)	$\frac{12}{100}$ = 0.12 (D)
$\frac{83}{100}$ = 0.83 (W)	$\frac{42}{100}$ = 0.42 (S)
$\frac{4}{10}$ = 0.4 (T)	$\frac{63}{100}$ = 0.63 (W)

To solve the riddle, write the circled letter in the matching blank.

Because T H E Y   D O N ' T
0.59 0.9 0.98   0.60 0.20 0.15 0.4

K N O W   T H E   W O R D S !
0.05 0.18 0.46 0.83 0.10 0.12 0.98 0.83 0.52 0.5 0.60 0.42 0.75

Gotta Be Picky!

Name _____ Date _____

Color the eggs in each nest that have equivalent decimals.

0.6 | 0.60 | 0.06
16.1 | 16.01 | 16.10
3.09 | 3.9 | 3.90
2.05 | 2.50 | 2.5
1.7 | 1.70 | 1.07
0.4 | 0.400 | 0.04
9.200 | 0.02 | 0.2
3.30 | 3.03 | 3.3
90.4 | 90.04 | 90.400
87.6 | 87.60 | 87.06

16 Equivalent decimals

Love at First Sight!

Name _____ Date _____

If the decimals are correctly ordered from least to greatest, color the milk or cookie.

2.31 6.5 9.86 | 45.07 45.57 45.7 | 5.2 5.17 4.95 | 23.0 57.8 41.03
0.82 0.81 0.80 | 1.7 1.3 1.0 | 7.68 7.8 8.06 8.7 | 13.94 13.95 14.94
17.09 17.90 17.89 | 0.08 0.9 8.0 | 0.21 0.27 0.22 | 6.53 6.35 6.30
5.40 5.41 5.39 | 2.01 2.05 2.07 | 18.99 19.10 19.19 | 61.73 64.82 64.87 64.99

Ordering decimals to hundredths **19**

Pulling Up the Plants

Name _____ Date _____

Round the decimals on the carrots to the nearest tenth.
Round the decimals on the turnips to the nearest hundredth.

18.68 = 18.7 | 469.386 = 469.39 | 175.043 = 175.04 | 129.56 = 129.6
93.614 = 93.61 | 312.05 = 312.1 | 16.987 = 16.99 | 76.43 = 76.4
93.72 = 93.7 | 88.705 = 88.71 | 4.71 = 4.7 | 10.410 = 10.41
12.655 = 12.66 | 66.67 = 66.7 | 50.044 = 50.04 | 3,014.28 = 3,014.3

22 Rounding decimals to the nearest tenth or hundredth

Underwater Surprise

Name _____ Date _____

Compare the decimals.
Write <, >, or = in each blank.
Color by the code.

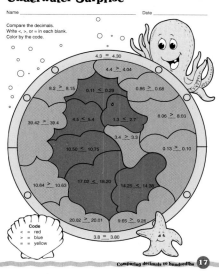

4.3 = 4.30
4.4 > 4.04
8.2 > 8.15
0.11 < 0.29
0.86 > 0.68
39.42 > 39.4
4.5 < 5.4
1.3 < 2.7
8.06 > 8.03
3.4 > 3.3
10.50 < 10.75
0.13 > 0.10
10.64 > 10.63
17.02 < 18.20
14.25 < 14.38
20.02 > 20.01
9.65 > 9.24
3.8 = 3.80

Code
< = red
> = blue
= = yellow

Comparing decimals to hundredths **17**

Who's the Skateboard Superstar?

Name _____ Date _____

Order the decimals from least to greatest.
Color the matching boxes to show the path
to the skateboard superstar.

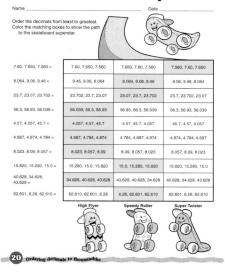

7.60, 7.650, 7.560 =	7.60, 7.650, 7.560	7.650, 7.60, 7.560	7.560, 7.60, 7.650
8.064, 9.06, 9.46 =	8.064, 9.06, 9.46	8.064, 9.06, 9.46	9.06, 9.46, 8.064
23.7, 23.07, 23.702 =	23.702, 23.7, 23.07	23.07, 23.7, 23.702	23.7, 23.702, 23.07
56.3, 56.93, 56.039 =	56.039, 56.3, 56.93	56.93, 56.3, 56.039	56.3, 56.93, 56.039
4.57, 4.057, 45.7 =	4.057, 4.57, 45.7	4.57, 45.7, 4.057	45.7, 4.57, 4.057
4.687, 4.874, 4.784 =	4.687, 4.784, 4.874	4.784, 4.687, 4.874	4.874, 4.784, 4.687
8.023, 8.09, 8.057 =	8.023, 8.057, 8.09	8.09, 8.057, 8.023	8.057, 8.09, 8.023
15.820, 15.280, 15.0 =	15.280, 15.0, 15.820	15.0, 15.280, 15.820	15.820, 15.280, 15.0
40.628, 34.628, 43.628 =	34.628, 40.628, 43.628	43.628, 40.628, 34.628	40.628, 34.628, 43.628
62.601, 6.26, 62.610 =	62.610, 62.601, 6.26	6.26, 62.601, 62.610	62.601, 6.26, 62.610

High Flyer | Speedy Roller | Super Twister

20 Ordering decimals to thousandths

Monkey Business

Name _____ Date _____

Add.

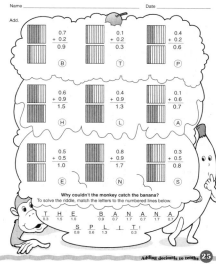

0.7 + 0.2 = 0.9 (B)
0.1 + 0.2 = 0.3 (T)
0.4 + 0.2 = 0.6 (P)
0.6 + 0.9 = 1.5 (H)
0.4 + 0.9 = 1.3 (L)
0.1 + 0.6 = 0.7 (A)
0.5 + 0.5 = 1.0 (E)
0.8 + 0.9 = 1.7 (N)
0.3 + 0.5 = 0.8 (S)

Why couldn't the monkey catch the banana?
To solve the riddle, match the letters on the numbered lines below.

T H E   B A N A N A
0.3 __ __   __ __ __ __ __ __

S P L I T
0.8 0.6 1.3   0.3

Adding decimals to tenths **25**

What's Ashore?

Name _____ Date _____

Compare the decimals.
Color blue if correct.
To solve the riddle, write the colored letters in order
in the blanks below.

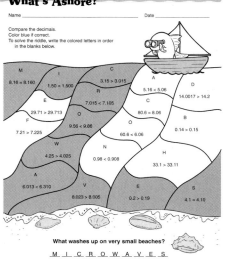

M 8.16 = 8.160
I 1.50 = 1.500
C 3.15 > 3.015
A 5.16 < 5.06
D 14.0017 > 14.2
R 7.015 < 7.105
E 29.71 > 29.713
C 80.6 = 8.06
B 0.14 > 0.15
O 9.56 < 9.86
O 60.6 < 6.06
7.21 > 7.225
W 4.25 > 4.025
N 0.98 < 0.908
H 33.1 > 33.11
A 6.013 < 6.310
V 8.023 > 8.005
E 0.2 > 0.19
S 4.1 = 4.10

What washes up on very small beaches?
M I C R O W A V E S

18 Comparing decimals to thousandths

Home Run Balls

Name _____ Date _____

Round each decimal to the nearest whole number.
Cross off the answer on the bat.
Some of the answers will not be crossed off.

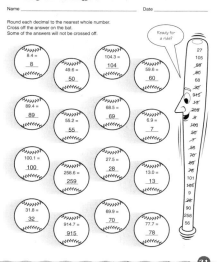

8.4 = 8 | 104.3 = 104 | 59.6 = 60
49.6 = 50 | |
89.4 = 89 | 68.5 = 69 | 6.9 = 7
55.2 = 55 | |
100.1 = 100 | 27.5 = 28 | 13.0 = 13
258.6 = 259 | |
31.8 = 32 | 69.9 = 70 | 77.7 = 78
914.7 = 915 | |

Ready for a ride?

27 105 65 66 68 915 15 258 8 100 7 55 70 89 26 28 101 10 9 28 90 258 56

Rounding decimals to the nearest whole number **21**

Cody the Cowboy Cat

Name _____ Date _____

Add.
Cross out the matching answer on the lasso.

5.7 + 1.1 = 6.8 | 4.7 + 2.4 = 7.1 | 8.0 + 4.3 = 12.3 | 2.6 + 2.2 = 4.8
3.5 + 1.2 = 4.7 | 0.1 + 2.8 = 2.9 | 8.3 + 0.5 = 8.8 | 4.3 + 6.2 = 10.5
3.3 + 1.2 = 4.5 | 8.2 + 6.1 = 14.3 | 0.7 + 3.5 = 4.2 | 4.4 + 3.2 = 7.6
7.5 + 2.4 = 9.9 | 7.8 + 2.5 = 10.3 | 10.9 + 4.0 = 14.9 | 22.6 + 8.6 = 31.2
11.5 + 1.3 = 12.8 | 4.9 + 5.1 = 10.0 | 15.9 + 2.2 = 18.1 |
40.4 + 1.3 = 41.7 | 2.6 + 5.1 = 7.7 | 7.6 + 1.4 = 9.0 |

26 Adding mixed decimals to tenths

Sweet Success!

Name _____ Date _____

Add.
Show your work on another sheet of paper.
Color each pair of matching jelly beans a different color.

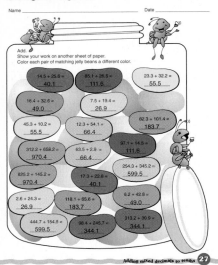

14.5 + 25.6 = **40.1**

85.1 + 26.5 = **111.6**

23.3 + 32.2 = **55.5**

16.4 + 32.6 = **49.0**

7.5 + 19.4 = **26.9**

45.3 + 10.2 = **55.5**

12.3 + 54.1 = **66.4**

82.3 + 101.4 = **183.7**

312.2 + 658.2 = **970.4**

63.5 + 2.9 = **66.4**

97.1 + 14.5 = **111.6**

825.2 + 145.2 = **970.4**

17.3 + 22.8 = **40.1**

254.3 + 345.2 = **599.5**

2.6 + 24.3 = **26.9**

118.1 + 65.6 = **183.7**

6.2 + 42.8 = **49.0**

444.7 + 154.8 = **599.5**

98.4 + 245.7 = **344.1**

313.2 + 30.9 = **344.1**

27 Adding mixed decimals to tenths

Unidentified Vacation Land

Name _____ Date _____

Add.
Show your work on another sheet of paper.
Color by the code.

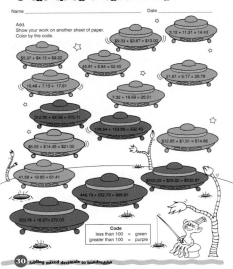

3.12 + 11.31 = 14.43

$9.33 + $3.67 = $13.00

$5.07 + $4.15 = $9.22

45.91 + 6.54 = 52.45

21.61 + 5.17 = 26.78

10.46 + 7.13 = 17.61

7.32 + 18.69 = 26.01

312.85 + 62.26 = 375.11

178.84 + 153.80 = 332.43

$12.95 + $1.91 = $14.86

$6.55 + $14.45 = $21.00

41.58 + 19.83 = 61.41

$503.25 + $29.62 = $532.87

446.18 + 552.73 = 998.91

253.76 + 18.27 = 272.03

Code
less than 100 = green
greater than 100 = purple

30 Adding mixed decimals to hundredths

Winded Wolf

Name _____ Date _____

Add.
Show your work.
Cross out the matching answer on the house.
The first one has been done for you.

6.35	7.50	8.61	5.80	1.47
+ 4.20	+ 2.27	+ 4.30	+ 3.14	+ 0.50
10.55	9.77	12.91	8.94	1.97

4.66	5.91	9.60	7.30
+ 2.70	+ 2.40	+ 0.04	+ 7.19
7.36	8.31	9.64	14.49

3.00	8.42	11.73	23.85
+ 2.47	+ 0.80	+ 4.10	+ 6.50
5.47	9.22	15.83	30.35

34.51	19.60	46.70	10.95
+ 9.50	+ 0.82	+ 8.68	+ 4.80
44.01	20.42	55.38	15.75

14.82	32.99
+ 12.20	+ 10.60
27.02	43.59

41.72
+ 30.00
71.72

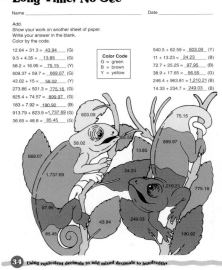

House numbers: 44.01, 9.64, 0.37, 12.91, 15.83, 7.36, 8.95, 9.28, 3.84, 15.75, 10.85, 5.47, 20.42, 43.59, 8.31, 14.49, 55.38, 27.02, 71.72, 30.35

THIS BUILDING MADE BY
3 PIGS CONSTRUCTION

33 Using equivalent decimals to add mixed decimals to hundredths

3, 2, 1—Zzzz!

Name _____ Date _____

Add.

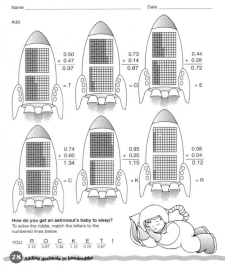

0.50	0.73	0.44
+ 0.47	+ 0.14	+ 0.28
0.97	0.87	0.72
= T	= O	= E

0.74	0.95	0.08
+ 0.60	+ 0.20	+ 0.04
1.34	1.15	0.12
= C	= K	= R

How do you get an astronaut's baby to sleep?
To solve the riddle, match the letters to the numbered lines below.

YOU R O C K E T !
 0.12 0.97 1.34 1.15 0.72 0.87 0.97

28 Adding decimals to hundredths

Dr. Callie Coe, Veterinarian

Name _____ Date _____

Add.

What did the veterinarian keep outside her door?

Mouse Medicine

3.215	13.059	65.834	8.573
+ 2.147	+ 7.338	+ 25.492	+ 4.586
5.362	20.397	91.326	13.159
= E	= T	= O	= E

53.864	75.926	657.712	531.754
+ 44.265	+ 19.157	+ 142.971	+ 289.687
98.129	95.083	800.683	821.441
= M	= L	= C	= T

126.391	331.408	407.318	38.965
+ 66.023	+ 278.649	+ 17.269	+ 15.317
192.414	610.057	424.587	54.282
= A	= U	= W	= M

To solve the riddle, match the letters to the numbered lines below.

A W E L C O M E   M U T T
192.414 54.282 610.057 821.441 20.397

31 Adding mixed decimals to thousandths

Long Time, No See

Name _____ Date _____

Add.
Show your work on another sheet of paper.
Write your answer in the blank.
Color by the code.

12.64 + 31.3 = _43.94_ (G)
9.5 + 4.35 = _13.85_ (G)
58.2 + 16.95 = _75.15_ (Y)
609.37 + 59.7 = _669.07_ (G)
43.02 + 15 = _58.02_ (Y)
273.86 + 501.3 = _775.16_ (G)
825.4 + 74.57 = _899.97_ (G)
183 + 7.92 = _190.92_ (B)
913.79 + 823.9 = _1,737.69_ (G)
36.65 + 48.8 = _85.45_ (G)

540.5 + 62.59 = _603.09_ (Y)
11 + 13.23 = _24.23_ (B)
72.7 + 25.25 = _97.95_ (B)
38.9 + 17.65 = _56.55_ (G)
246.4 + 963.81 = _1,210.21_ (B)
14.33 + 234.7 = _249.03_ (B)

Color Code
G = green
B = brown
Y = yellow

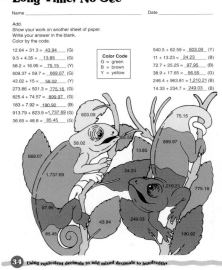

Numbers on leaves: 603.09, 75.15, 58.02, 56.55, 13.85, 899.97, 669.07, 1,737.69, 24.23, 1,210.21, 775.16, 97.95, 249.03, 43.94, 85.45, 190.92

34 Using equivalent decimals to add mixed decimals to hundredths

Crazy-Colored Cow

Name _____ Date _____

Add.
Color by the code.

15.16	55.84
+ 15.39	+ 6.27
30.55	62.11

7.32	37.66
+ 5.08	+ 4.08
12.40	41.74

78.83
+ 65.96
144.79

35.99	20.29	73.73
+ 26.41	+ 4.18	+ 9.54
62.40	24.47	83.27

14.64	44.59
+ 11.34	+ 5.33
25.96	49.92

85.95	95.77
+ 28.63	+ 42.89
114.58	138.66

9.17	16.09
+ 7.33	+ 4.06
16.50	20.15

30.58	71.72
+ 15.22	+ 17.64
45.80	89.36

30.62
+ 29.49
60.11

28.39
+ 14.29
42.68

22.31	48.85
+ 1.02	+ 8.23
23.33	57.08

Code
0–25 = red
25.01–50 = blue
50.01–100 = green
100–150 = yellow

29 Adding mixed decimals to hundredths

Freestyle Armadillo

Name _____ Date _____

Add.
Show your work on another sheet of paper.
Color if correct.

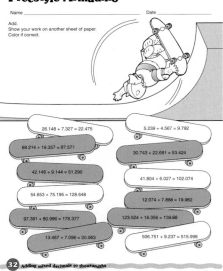

26.148 + 7.327 = 22.475

5.239 + 4.567 = 9.792

68.214 + 19.357 = 87.571

30.743 + 22.681 = 53.424

42.146 + 9.144 = 51.290

41.804 + 6.027 = 102.074

54.653 + 75.195 = 128.648

12.074 + 7.888 = 19.962

97.381 + 80.996 = 178.377

123.524 + 16.356 = 139.88

13.467 + 7.096 = 20.563

506.751 + 9.237 = 515.998

32 Adding mixed decimals to thousandths

Orange Outing

Name _____ Date _____

Add.
Show your work.

Why didn't the orange cross the road?

	168.50	41.67	31.700
	+ 1.24	+ 3.70	+ 2.549
	169.74	45.37	34.249
	= B	= I	= C

	59.620	5.00	88.40
	+ 4.099	+ 6.05	+ 73.51
	63.719	11.05	161.91
	= E	= T	= A

208.87	346.100	54.22	519.253
+ 2.20	+ 50.334	+ 8.50	+ 443.600
211.07	396.434	62.72	962.853
= S	= R	= U	= E

16.740	6,816.40	7.175	61.476	262.500	72.93
+ 5.479	+ 629.54	+ 6.830	+ 12.930	+ 8.796	+ 78.90
22.219	7,445.94	14.005	74.406	271.296	151.83
= I	= E	= E	= C	= A	= U

6.120	515.18	91.29	3,951.40	700.148	49.17
+ 1.982	+ 94.50	+ 18.00	+ 795.98	+ 23.650	+ 28.70
8.102	609.68	109.29	4,747.38	723.798	77.87
= O	= N	= U	= F	= T	= U

To solve the riddle, match the letters to the numbered lines below.

B E C A U S E   I T   R A N
169.74 45.37 211.07 962.853 151.83 271.296   45.37 11.05   396.434 161.91 609.68

O U T   O F   J U I C E !
8.102 723.798   271.296 4,747.38   77.87 74.406 109.29 7,445.94

35 Using equivalent decimals to add mixed decimals to thousandths

What's for Lunch?

Name _____ Date _____

Add.
Show your work on another sheet of paper.
Color the answer to reveal the path to the seal's lunch.

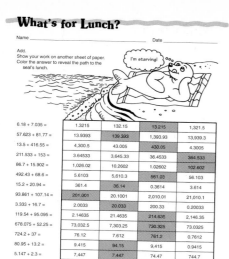

I'm starving!

6.18 + 7.035 =	1.3215	132.15	**13.215**	1,321.5
57.623 + 81.77 =	13.9393	**139.393**	1,393.93	13,939.3
13.5 + 416.55 =	4,300.5	43.005	**430.05**	4.3005
211.533 + 153 =	3.64533	3,645.33	**364.533**	364.533
86.7 + 15.902 =	1,026.02	10.2602	**1.02602**	102.602
492.43 + 68.6 =	5.6103	5,610.3	**561.03**	56.103
15.2 + 20.94 =	361.4	**36.14**	0.3614	3.614
93.861 + 107.14 =	**201.001**	20.1001	2,010.01	21,010.1
3.333 + 16.7 =	2.0033	**20.033**	200.33	0.20033
119.54 + 95.095 =	2.14635	21.4635	**214.635**	2,146.35
678.075 + 52.25 =	73,032.5	7,303.25	**730.325**	73.0325
724.2 + 37 =	76.12	7.612	**761.2**	0.7612
80.95 + 13.2 =	9.415	**94.15**	9,415	0.9415
5.147 + 2.3 =	**7.447**	7.447	74.47	744.7

36 — Using equivalent decimals to add mixed decimals to thousandths

---

Friends at the Food Court

Name _____ Date _____

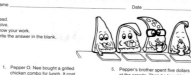

Read.
Solve.
Show your work.
Write the answer in the blank.

1. Pepper O. Nee bought a grilled chicken combo for lunch. It cost $4.59. She also bought a cherry slush for $1.67. How much did Pepper spend in all?
   $ __6.26__

2. Pepper's best friend, Olive, bought a taco salad for $5.39 and a medium soda for $1.26. How much did Olive's lunch cost in all?
   $ __6.65__

3. Pepper's sister bought a double cheeseburger for $3.89. Her french fries cost $1.39. How much did Pepper's sister spend in all?
   $ __5.28__

4. Pepper spent $8.45 on food at the mall. Pepper's brother and sister spent $7.01 on their food. How much in all did Pepper, her brother, and her sister spend on food?
   $ __15.46__

5. Pepper's brother spent five dollars at the arcade. Then he bought a slice of pizza for $1.73. How much did Pepper's brother spend in all?
   $ __6.73__

6. Pepper's cousin ordered the chicken stir-fry. It cost $4.85. He also bought a bottle of water for two dollars. How much did Pepper's cousin spend all together?
   $ __6.85__

7. Pepper and Olive each bought cookies after lunch. Pepper's cookie cost $2.19 and Olive's cost $1.38. How much did their cookies cost in all?
   $ __3.57__

8. Pepper's cousin bought an ice-cream cone for $2.46. He also bought a pack of gum for $1.87. How much did Pepper's cousin spend on ice cream and gum?
   $ __4.33__

Story problems: adding mixed decimals to hundredths — 39

Drumming Dragon

Name _____ Date _____

Subtract.
Show your work.

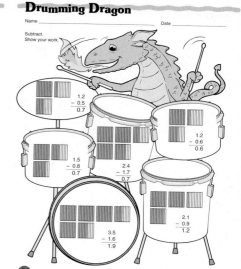

$$1.2 - 0.5 = 0.7$$

$$1.2 - 0.6 = 0.6$$

$$1.5 - 0.8 = 0.7$$

$$2.4 - 1.7 = 0.7$$

$$3.5 - 1.6 = 1.9$$

$$2.1 - 0.9 = 1.2$$

44 — Subtracting mixed decimals to tenths

"Cell-ebrities"

Name _____ Date _____

Add.
Show your work on another sheet of paper.
Write each answer in the magic square. The sum of each row and column should equal 350.

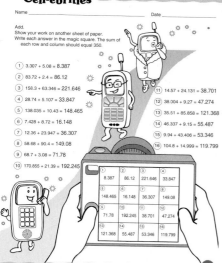

1. 3.307 + 5.08 = 8.387
2. 83.72 + 2.4 = 86.12
3. 156.3 + 63.346 = 221.646
4. 28.74 + 5.107 = 33.847
5. 138.035 + 10.43 = 148.465
6. 7.428 + 8.72 = 16.148
7. 12.36 + 23.947 = 36.307
8. 58.68 + 90.4 = 149.08
9. 68.7 + 3.08 = 71.78
10. 170.855 + 21.39 = 192.245
11. 14.57 + 24.131 = 38.701
12. 38.004 + 9.27 = 47.274
13. 35.51 + 85.858 = 121.368
14. 46.337 + 9.15 = 55.487
15. 9.94 + 43.406 = 53.346
16. 104.8 + 14.999 = 119.799

(1)	(2)	(3)	(4)
8.387	86.12	221.646	33.847
148.465	16.148	36.307	149.08
71.78	192.245	38.701	47.274
121.368	55.487	53.346	119.799

Using equivalent decimals to add mixed decimals to thousandths — 37

Fiddler Crab Quartet

Name _____ Date _____

Read.
Solve each problem on a separate sheet of paper.
Write the answer in the blank.

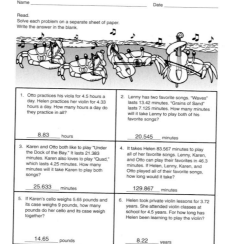

1. Otto practices his viola for 4.5 hours a day. Helen practices her violin for 4.33 hours a day. How many hours a day do they practice in all?
   __8.83__ hours

2. Lenny has two favorite songs. "Waves" lasts 13.42 minutes. "Grains of Sand" lasts 7.125 minutes. How many minutes will it take Lenny to play both of his favorite songs?
   __20.545__ minutes

3. Karen and Otto both like to play "Under the Dock of the Bay." It lasts 21.383 minutes. Karen also loves to play "Quad," which lasts 4.25 minutes. How many minutes will it take Karen to play both songs?
   __25.633__ minutes

4. It takes Helen 83.567 minutes to play all of her favorite songs. Lenny, Karen, and Otto can play their favorites in 46.3 minutes. If Helen, Lenny, Karen, and Otto played all of their favorite songs, how long would it take?
   __129.867__ minutes

5. If Karen's cello weighs 5.65 pounds and its case weighs 9 pounds, how many pounds do her cello and its case weigh together?
   __14.65__ pounds

6. Helen took private violin lessons for 3.72 years. She attended violin classes at school for 4.5 years. For how long has Helen been learning to play the violin?
   __8.22__ years

40 — Story problems: using equivalent decimals to add mixed decimals to thousandths

---

Stop and Smell the Roses

Name _____ Date _____

Subtract.
Show your work.
Write each answer in the magic square.
The sum of each row and column should equal 300.

$$7.5 - 3.6 = 3.9$$

$$12.2 - 4.8 = 7.4$$

$$50.3 - 19.4 = 30.9$$

$$322.6 - 64.8 = 257.8$$

$$170.2 - 5.9 = 164.3$$

$$25.1 - 16.4 = 8.7$$

$$480.3 - 358.9 = 121.4$$

$$63.4 - 57.8 = 5.6$$

$$826.1 - 745.9 = 80.2$$

$$254.0 - 121.9 = 132.1$$

$$99.1 - 24.9 = 74.2$$

$$108.2 - 94.7 = 13.5$$

$$512.4 - 460.8 = 51.6$$

$$961.3 - 809.5 = 151.8$$

$$79.4 - 5.9 = 73.5$$

$$745.0 - 721.9 = 23.1$$

ROSES

3.9	7.4	30.9	257.8
164.3	8.7	121.4	5.6
80.2	132.1	74.2	13.5
51.6	151.8	73.5	23.1

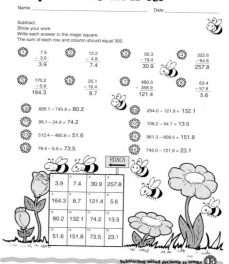

Subtracting mixed decimals to tenths — 45

Weather Watch

Name _____ Date _____

Read.
Solve.
Show your work.
Write the answer in the blank.

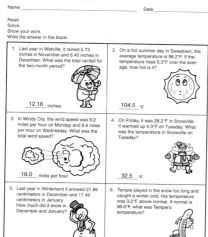

1. Last year in Wetville, it rained 5.73 inches in November and 6.45 inches in December. What was the total rainfall for the two-month period?
   __12.18__ inches

2. On a hot summer day in Sweatown, the average temperature is 98.2°F. If the temperature rises 6.3°F over the average, how hot is it?
   __104.5__ °F

3. In Windy City, the wind speed was 9.2 miles per hour on Monday and 8.8 miles per hour on Wednesday. What was the total wind speed?
   __18.0__ miles per hour

4. On Friday, it was 28.2°F in Snowville. It warmed up 4.3°F on Tuesday. What was the temperature in Snowville on Tuesday?
   __32.5__ °F

5. Last year in Winterland it snowed 21.85 centimeters in December and 17.49 centimeters in January. How much did it snow in December and January?
   __39.34__ centimeters

6. Tempie played in the snow too long and caught a winter cold. His temperature was 3.2°F above normal. If normal is 98.6°F, what was Tempie's temperature?
   __101.8__ °F

38 — Story problems: adding mixed decimals to hundredths

Apple Delight!

Name _____ Date _____

Subtract.
Show your work.

$$0.7 - 0.3 = 0.4$$

$$0.9 - 0.1 = 0.8$$

$$0.8 - 0.6 = 0.2$$

$$0.9 - 0.4 = 0.5$$

$$0.4 - 0.2 = 0.2$$

$$0.6 - 0.3 = 0.3$$

$$0.7 - 0.5 = 0.2$$

$$0.9 - 0.4 = 0.5$$

$$0.4 - 0.3 = 0.1$$

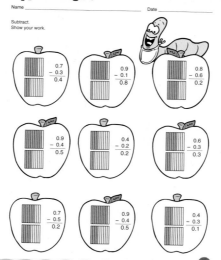

Subtracting decimals to tenths — 43

The Cat's Out of the Bag

Name _____ Date _____

Subtract.
Show your work.

(A) $$9.84 - 2.43 = 7.41$$

(T) $$24.63 - 13.48 = 11.15$$

(Y) $$87.52 - 35.47 = 52.05$$

(H) $$17.94 - 6.26 = 11.68$$

(S) $$34.23 - 3.49 = 30.74$$

(I) $$9.74 - 5.05 = 4.69$$

(T) $$21.36 - 18.47 = 2.89$$

(E) $$43.77 - 8.42 = 35.35$$

(H) $$84.03 - 62.74 = 21.29$$

(E) $$65.72 - 4.38 = 61.34$$

(V) $$7.04 - 3.99 = 3.05$$

(E) $$64.22 - 27.61 = 36.61$$

(N) $$93.42 - 13.76 = 79.66$$

(T) $$25.18 - 11.79 = 13.39$$

(K) $$74.88 - 9.99 = 64.89$$

(I) $$32.47 - 28.55 = 3.92$$

What do cats have that no other animals have?
To solve the riddle, match the letters above to the numbered lines below.

T	H	E	Y		H	A	V	E
11.15	21.29	35.35	52.05		11.68	7.41	3.05	35.35

K	I	T	T	E	N	S	!
64.89	4.69	13.39	2.89	61.34	79.66	30.74	3.92

46 — Subtracting mixed decimals to hundredths

Balancing Act

Name _____ Date _____

Subtract.
Show your work on another sheet of paper.
Color by the code.

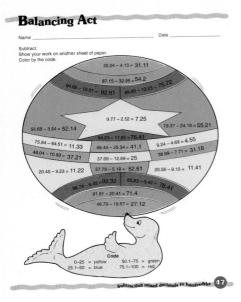

35.24 – 4.13 = 31.11

87.15 – 32.95 = 54.2

94.82 – 12.01 = 82.81   86.95 – 13.23 = 75.72

9.77 – 2.52 = 7.25

55.68 – 3.54 = 52.14   79.37 – 24.16 = 55.21

75.84 – 64.51 = 11.33   94.23 – 17.82 = 76.41   9.24 – 4.69 = 4.55

48.04 – 10.83 = 37.21   66.44 – 25.34 = 41.1   37.69 – 12.69 = 25   38.89 – 7.71 = 31.18

20.45 – 9.23 = 11.22   57.79 – 5.18 = 52.61   20.56 – 9.15 = 11.41

98.74 – 6.42 = 92.32   85.83 – 9.42 = 76.41

91.81 – 20.41 = 71.4

46.79 – 19.67 = 27.12

Code
0–25 = yellow   50.1–75 = green
25.1–50 = blue   75.1–100 = red

Subtracting mixed decimals to hundredths **47**

Have a (Beach) Ball!

Name _____ Date _____

Subtract.
Show your work.
The first one has been started for you.

14.50
– 3.07
11.43

36.60
– 25.11
11.49

9.75
– 6.40
3.35

18.80
– 4.51
14.29

24.50
– 3.23
21.27

12.48
– 1.30
11.18

8.74
– 8.10
0.64

65.84
– 4.60
61.24

224.70
– 124.62
100.08

5.80
– 4.61
1.19

40.70
– 20.53
20.17

16.42
– 6.20
10.22

742.90
– 31.75
711.15

180.63
– 10.40
170.23

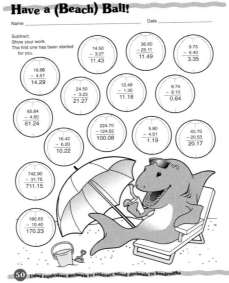

50 Using equivalent decimals to subtract mixed decimals to hundredths

Searching High and Low

Name _____ Date _____

Subtract.
Show your work on another sheet.

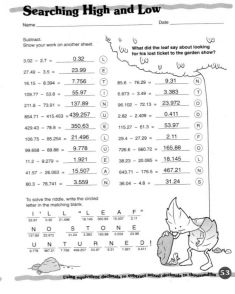

What did the leaf say about looking for his lost ticket to the garden show?

3.02 – 2.7 = 0.32 (L)

27.49 – 3.5 = 23.99 (E)

16.15 – 8.394 = 7.756 (T)   85.6 – 76.29 = 9.31 (N)

109.77 – 53.8 = 55.97 (I)   6.873 – 3.49 = 3.383 (T)

211.8 – 73.91 = 137.89 (N)   96.102 – 72.13 = 23.972 (O)

854.71 – 415.453 = 439.257 (U)   2.82 – 2.409 = 0.411 (D)

429.43 – 78.8 = 350.63 (L)   115.27 – 61.3 = 53.97 (R)

106.75 – 85.254 = 21.496 (L)   29.4 – 27.29 = 2.11 (F)

99.658 – 89.88 = 9.778 (U)   726.6 – 560.72 = 165.88 (O)

11.2 – 9.279 = 1.921 (E)   38.23 – 20.085 = 18.145 (L)

41.57 – 26.063 = 15.507 (A)   643.71 – 176.5 = 467.21 (N)

80.3 – 76.741 = 3.559 (N)   36.04 – 4.8 = 31.24 (S)

To solve the riddle, write the circled letter in the matching blank.

I ' L L " L E A F "
55.97 .32 21.496 18.145 350.63 15.507 2.11

N O S T O N E
137.89 23.972 .32 3.383 165.88 3.559 23.99

U N T U R N E D !
9.778 467.21 7.756 439.257 53.97 9.31 1.921 0.411

Using equivalent decimals to subtract mixed decimals to thousandths **53**

Daydreamin'

Name _____ Date _____

Subtract.
Show your work on another sheet of paper.
Cross off the matching answer on the camel.

$5.92 – $2.28 = $3.64   73.84 – 9.56 = 64.28

42.30 – 5.67 = 36.63   121.41 – 65.32 = 56.09

8.06 – 3.19 = 4.87   57.30 – 36.59 = 20.71

500.25 – 0.67 = 499.58 $4.12 – $2.08 = $2.04

$96.51 – $61.23 = $35.28   69.73 – 21.54 = 48.19

7.11 – 6.88 = 0.23   304.67 – 40.49 = 264.18

412.34 – 198.25 = 214.09 $273.23 – $164.75 = $108.48

$915.45 – $67.09 = $848.36   80.60 – 17.87 = 62.73

3.76 – 2.87 = 0.89

$26.31 – $15.19 = $11.12

4.87   36.63   56.09
499.58 $35.28 $11.12
$108.48   0.23   264.18
64.28   48.19   62.73
20.71 $3.64 $2.04
$848.36   214.09   0.89

48 Subtracting mixed decimals to hundredths

Colorful Caterpillar

Name _____ Date _____

Subtract.
Show your work on another sheet of paper.
Color by the code.

Color Code
B = blue   R = red
Y = yellow   O = orange
G = green   P = purple

12.4 – 3.27 = 9.13 (B)

63.8 – 38.52 = 25.28 (P)   35.8 – 29.46 = 6.34 (B)

135.73 – 124.2 = 11.53 (G)   57.39 – 42.9 = 14.49 (O)

31.2 – 1.65 = 29.55 (B)   346.5 – 273.32 = 73.18 (Y)

290.4 – 184.66 = 105.74 (R)   152.6 – 140.78 = 11.82 (P)

208.25 – 3.6 = 204.65 (B)

25.4 – 1.37 = 24.03 (G)

378.46 – 259.2 = 119.26 (R)

21.3 – 15.28 = 6.02 (P)

17.9 – 10.31 = 7.59 (O)

24.63 – 15.4 = 9.23 (B)

40.7 – 38.11 = 2.59 (Y)

376.8 – 283.59 = 93.21 (O)

64.1 – 21.34 = 42.76 (O)

425.78 – 5.5 = 420.28 (Y)

119.2 – 84.15 = 35.05 (G)

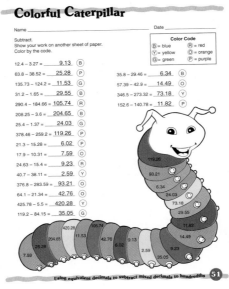

119.26
93.21
6.34
24.03
73.18
29.55
11.82
420.28   105.74   14.49
25.28   11.53   42.76   6.02   9.13   9.23
7.59   204.65   2.59   35.05

Using equivalent decimals to subtract mixed decimals to hundredths **51**

Meeting at the Movies

Name _____ Date _____

Read.
Solve.
Show your work.
Write the answer in the blank.

TICKETS

1. It costs $8.25 to go to the movies in the evening. One ticket to the afternoon show only costs $4.50. How much can Macy save by going to the movies in the afternoon instead of in the evening?
$3.75

2. Morris has $10.37. If he buys a ticket to the afternoon show for $4.50, how much will he have left?
$5.87

3. Mel has $9.52. If she spends $4.50 on her ticket, how much will she have left?
$5.02

4. Max found $3.73 in his backpack. How much more money does he need to buy a $4.50 ticket to the afternoon show?
$0.77

5. Max, Mel, Macy, and Morris are going to the afternoon to watch the latest episode of M-Men! All together, Max, Mel, Macy, and Morris have $35.64. Their tickets cost $18.40. How much money do they have left?
$17.24

6. If Max, Mel, Macy, and Morris had gone to the evening showing instead of the afternoon show, their tickets would have cost $33.00. How much of their $35.64 would they have had left?
$2.64

54 Story problems: subtracting mixed decimals to hundredths

Lily Pad Leap

Name _____ Date _____

Subtract.
Color if correct to show the path to the other side of the pond.

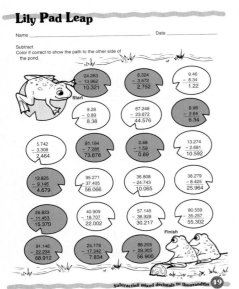

24.283
– 13.962
10.321

6.324
– 3.572
2.752

9.46
– 8.34
1.22

Start

9.28
– 0.89
8.38

67.248
– 23.672
44.576

8.98
– 2.64
6.34

5.742
– 3.308
2.464

81.164
– 7.286
73.878

2.48
– 1.59
0.89

13.274
– 2.681
10.592

13.825
– 9.146
4.679

95.271
– 37.405
56.066

36.808
– 24.743
10.065

38.279
– 8.425
25.964

26.823
– 11.453
15.370

40.909
– 18.707
22.002

57.145
– 36.928
30.217

80.559
– 35.257
55.302

91.146
– 22.234
68.912

25.176
– 17.342
7.834

86.205
– 29.305
56.900

Finish

Subtracting mixed decimals to thousandths **49**

"Salamand-air"

Name _____ Date _____

Subtract.
Show your work on another sheet.
Cross off each matching answer in the answer bank.

86.06 – 13.4 = 72.66   88.99 – 79.3 = 9.69

267.18 – 40.392 = 226.788   635.45 – 244.551 = 390.899

413.2 – 110.751 = 302.449   48.578 – 32.21 = 16.368

65.203 – 19.81 = 45.393   392.37 – 9.462 = 382.908

43.845 – 25.66 = 18.185   17.119 – 10.9 = 6.219

920.375 – 51.14 = 869.235   53.46 – 12.613 = 40.847

34.62 – 32.541 = 2.079

71.05 – 8.275 = 62.775

79.46 – 28.056 = 51.404

26.834 – 7.05 = 19.784

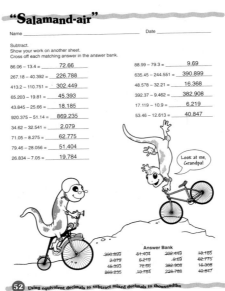

Look at me, Grandpa!

Answer Bank
390.899   51.404   302.449   18.185
2.079   6.219   9.69   62.775
45.393   72.66   382.908   16.368
869.235   19.784   226.788   40.847

52 Using equivalent decimals to subtract mixed decimals to thousandths

Race Day

Name _____ Date _____

Read.
Solve each problem on another sheet of paper.
Write the answer on the blanks.

On your mark...

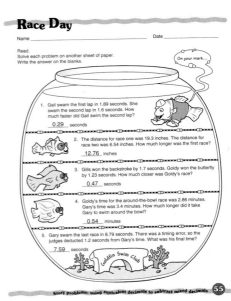

1. Gail swam the first lap in 1.89 seconds. She swam the second lap in 1.6 seconds. How much faster did Gail swim the second lap?
0.29 seconds

2. The distance for race one was 19.3 inches. The distance for race two was 6.54 inches. How much longer was the first race?
12.76 inches

3. Gills won the backstroke by 1.7 seconds. Goldy won the butterfly by 1.23 seconds. How much closer was Goldy's race?
0.47 seconds

4. Goldy's time for the around-the-bowl race was 2.86 minutes. Gary's time was 3.4 minutes. How much longer did it take Gary to swim around the bowl?
0.54 minutes

5. Gary swam the last race in 8.79 seconds. There was a timing error, so the judges deducted 1.2 seconds from Gary's time. What was his final time?
7.59 seconds

Goldfish Swim Club

Story problems: using equivalent decimals to subtract mixed decimals **55**

Recycleton, USA

Name _____ Date _____

Read.
Solve each problem on another sheet of paper.
Write the answer in the blank provided.

1. The recycling center has collected 515.6 tons of paper this year. Last year, the center collected 482.75 tons. How much more paper has been collected this year?
   __32.85__ tons

2. During the creek cleanup, 3,200.562 pounds of trash were cleaned up. Volunteers sorted out 853.78 pounds of the trash for recycling. How many pounds of trash were left?
   __2,346.782__ pounds

3. This month, 36.71 percent of the town recycled milk cartons. Last month, 23.5 percent did. What is the difference?
   __13.21__ percent

4. Of the 2,500 pounds of aluminum cans sold in Recycleton, 1,276.33 pounds were recycled. How many pounds were not recycled?
   __1,223.67__ pounds

5. Of the plastic recycled this year, 71.83 percent was type 2 plastic. Type 1 plastic made up 16.079 percent. What is the difference?
   __55.751__ percent

6. It cost 15.8 million dollars to run the recycling center last year. This year, it has cost 14.259 million dollars. How much less has it cost this year?
   __1.541__ million dollars

56 Story problems: using equivalent decimals to subtract mixed decimals

Banana Bandit

Name _____ Date _____

Multiply.
Show your work on another sheet of paper.
Color yellow if correct to show how many bananas the monkey stole.

0.6 x 6 = 0.36
0.21 x 5 = 10.5
0.85 x 6 = 0.51
412 x 0.7 = 28.84
0.86 x 3 = 2.58
620 x 0.9 = 55.8
242 x 0.2 = 48.4
0.4 x 8 = 3.2
0.47 x 58 = 27.26
99 x 0.8 = 79.2
782 x 0.4 = 31.28
0.76 x 7 = 5.32
58 x 0.5 = 29.0
0.22 x 9 = 19.8
501 x 0.18 = 90.18
0.68 x 7 = 47.6
0.37 x 4 = 1.48
0.29 x 33 = 9.57
0.7 x 3 = 0.21

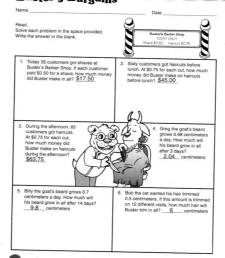

61 Multiplying decimals to hundredths by whole numbers

Heard the Skunk's Joke?

Name _____ Date _____

Multiply.
Show your work.
Color each shape that contains a correct answer.

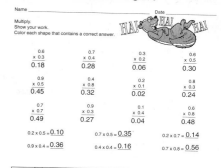

0.6 x 0.3 = 0.18	0.7 x 0.4 = 0.28	0.3 x 0.2 = 0.06	0.6 x 0.5 = 0.30
0.9 x 0.5 = 0.45	0.4 x 0.8 = 0.32	0.2 x 0.1 = 0.02	0.8 x 0.3 = 0.24
0.7 x 0.7 = 0.49	0.9 x 0.3 = 0.27	0.1 x 0.4 = 0.04	0.6 x 0.8 = 0.48

0.2 x 0.5 = __0.10__   0.7 x 0.5 = __0.35__   0.2 x 0.7 = __0.14__
0.9 x 0.4 = __0.36__   0.4 x 0.4 = __0.16__   0.7 x 0.8 = __0.56__

64 Multiplying decimals to tenths

Emergency!

Name _____ Date _____

Add.
Show your work.
To solve the riddle, color the matching letter.

0.7 x 3 = 2.1
315 x 0.2 = 63.0
0.9 x 8 = 7.2
46 x 0.4 = 18.4
0.2 x 9 = 1.8

37 x 0.5 = 18.5
0.3 x 8 = 2.4
116 x 0.7 = 81.2
0.5 x 5 = 2.5
12 x 0.4 = 4.8

25 x 0.8 = 20.0
73 x 0.6 = 43.8
0.6 x 6 = 3.6
44 x 0.9 = 39.6
0.4 x 3 = 1.2

Why did the book go to the hospital?

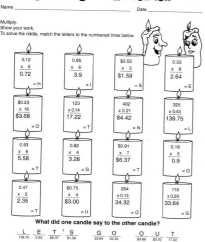

59 Multiplying decimals to tenths by whole numbers

Buster's Bargains

Name _____ Date _____

Read.
Solve each problem in the space provided.
Write the answer in the blank.

Buster's Barber Shop
TODAY ONLY!
Shave $0.50   Haircut $0.75

1. Today 35 customers got shaves at Buster's Barber Shop. If each customer paid $0.50 for a shave, how much money did Buster make in all? __$17.50__

2. Sixty customers got haircuts before lunch. At $0.75 for each cut, how much money did Buster make on haircuts before lunch? __$45.00__

3. During the afternoon, 85 customers got haircuts. At $0.75 for each cut, how much money did Buster make on haircuts during the afternoon? __$63.75__

4. Greg the goat's beard grows 0.68 centimeters a day. How much will his beard grow in all after 3 days? __2.04__ centimeters

5. Billy the goat's beard grows 0.7 centimeters a day. How much will his beard grow in all after 14 days? __9.8__ centimeters

6. Bob the cat wanted his hair trimmed 0.5 centimeters. If this amount is trimmed on 12 different visits, how much hair will Buster trim in all? __6__ centimeters

62 Story problems: multiplying decimals to hundredths by whole numbers

"Snail-athon"

Name _____ Date _____

Multiply.
Show your work.

0.01K!

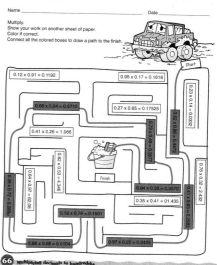

0.57 x 0.9 = 0.513
0.32 x 0.8 = 0.256
0.16 x 0.4 = 0.064
0.28 x 0.6 = 0.168
0.43 x 0.5 = 0.215
0.71 x 0.7 = 0.497
0.89 x 0.3 = 0.267
0.64 x 0.2 = 0.128
0.07 x 0.8 = 0.056
0.95 x 0.5 = 0.475
0.39 x 0.6 = 0.234
0.52 x 0.4 = 0.208
0.61 x 0.2 = 0.122
0.28 x 0.9 = 0.252
0.76 x 0.8 = 0.608
0.44 x 0.7 = 0.308

65 Multiplying decimals to hundredths

"En-light-ening" Conversation

Name _____ Date _____

Multiply.
Show your work.
To solve the riddle, match the letters to the numbered lines below.

0.12 x 6 = 0.72   = H
0.65 x 6 = 3.9   = I
$0.53 x 3 = $1.59   = S
0.33 x 8 = 2.64   = E

$0.23 x 16 = $3.68   = O
123 x 0.14 = 17.22   = T
402 x 0.21 = 84.42   = N
325 x 0.43 = 139.75   = L

0.93 x 6 = 5.58   = T
0.82 x 4 = 3.28   = G
$0.91 x 7 = $6.37   = T
0.18 x 5 = 0.9   = O

0.47 x 5 = 2.35   = T
$0.75 x 4 = $3.00   = U
264 x 0.13 = 34.32   = O
116 x 0.29 = 33.64   = O

What did one candle say to the other candle?

L E T ' S   G O   O U T
139.75 2.64 $6.37 $1.59   3.9   5.58 17.22

T O N I G H T !
5.58 .90   84.42 3.9   0.72   2.35

60 Multiplying decimals to hundredths by whole numbers

Roll It On!

Name _____ Date _____

Read.
Solve each problem on another sheet of paper.
Write the answer in the blank.

1. Robby Roller adds 0.3 ounces of tint to each gallon of brown paint. How many ounces of tint will he need to add for 65 gallons? __19.5__ ounces

2. Tina Tray has 8 gallons of paint. If she adds 0.72 ounces of tint to each gallon, how much tint will she add in all? __5.76__ ounces

3. Robby needs to add 0.49 ounces of tint to each gallon of red paint. How many ounces of tint will he need for 12 gallons? __5.88__ ounces

4. Tina has 235 gallons of green paint. If she adds 0.6 ounces of tint to each gallon, how much tint will she add in all? __141__ ounces

5. Robby adds 0.8 ounces of tint to each gallon of blue paint. If he tints 500 gallons, how much tint will he use in all? __400__ ounces

6. Tina has 47 gallons of purple paint. If she adds 0.26 ounces of tint to each gallon, how much tint will she use in all? __12.22__ ounces

63 Story Problems: multiplying decimals to hundredths by whole numbers

Bath Time!

Name _____ Date _____

Multiply.
Show your work on another sheet of paper.
Color if correct.
Connect all the colored boxes to draw a path to the finish.

0.12 x 0.91 = 0.1192
0.95 x 0.17 = 0.1616
0.23 x 0.14 = 0.0322
0.68 x 0.84 = 0.5712
0.27 x 0.65 = 0.17525
0.52 x 0.66 = 0.3472
0.41 x 0.26 = 1.066
0.75 x 0.49 = 0.3675
0.82 x 0.53 = 4.346
0.76 x 0.32 = 2.432
0.64 x 0.97 = 62.08
0.94 x 0.38 = 0.3572
0.43 x 0.72 = 0.3096
0.43 x 0.63 = 0.2580
0.35 x 0.41 = 0.1435
0.19 x 0.79 = 0.1501
0.88 x 0.58 = 0.5104
0.97 x 0.25 = 0.2425

66 Multiplying decimals to hundredths

139

Go for the Goal!

Name _____ Date _____

Multiply.
Show your work.
Color the boxes with answers greater than 25 to show the path to the goal.

Finish	6.7 ×4 = 26.8	3.7 ×7 = 25.9	9.8 ×9 = 88.2	16.8 ×3 = 50.4
3.4 ×4 = 13.6	1.6 ×2 = 3.2	7.3 ×3 = 21.9	2.3 ×7 = 16.1	8.2 ×5 = 41.0
4.7 ×8 = 37.6	11.7 ×3 = 35.1	12.4 ×6 = 74.4	5.6 ×9 = 50.4	10.4 ×6 = 62.4
13.2 ×2 = 26.4	2.9 ×4 = 11.6	4.5 ×5 = 22.5	3.6 ×3 = 10.8	1.8 ×7 = 12.6
8.6 ×6 = 51.6	7.2 ×5 = 36.0	9.4 ×4 = 37.6	Start	

"Whoo's" There?

Name _____ Date _____

Multiply.
Color by the code.

Color Code
0–25.00 = green
25.01–50.00 = brown
50.01–75.00 = yellow

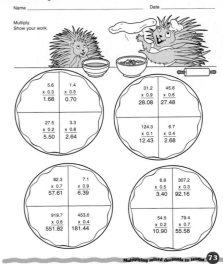

1.68 ×4 = 6.72
9.73 ×2 = 19.46
8.31 ×7 = 58.17
9.17 ×6 = 55.02
7.25 ×3 = 21.75
2.87 ×9 = 24.03
5.25 ×2 = 10.5
3.01 ×5 = 15.05
7.62 ×6 = 45.72
9.87 ×4 = 39.48
3.36 ×3 = 10.08
2.41 ×5 = 12.05
8.52 ×8 = 68.16
31.54 ×2 = 63.08
5.82 = 39.41
6.38 ×3 = 19.14
8.13 ×3 = 24.39
21.28 ×2 = 42.56
9.43 ×7 = 66.01
6.23 ×6 = 37.38
9.14 ×2 = 18.28
1.01 ×3 = 3.03
8.61 ×5 = 44.05
7.06 ×8 = 56.48
4.47 ×4 = 17.88

Prickly Pizza

Name _____ Date _____

Multiply.
Show your work.

5.6 ×0.3 = 1.68 | 1.4 ×0.5 = 0.70
31.2 ×0.9 = 28.08 | 45.8 ×0.6 = 27.48
27.5 ×0.2 = 5.50 | 3.3 ×0.8 = 2.64
124.3 ×0.1 = 12.43 | 6.7 ×0.4 = 2.68
82.3 ×0.7 = 57.61 | 7.1 ×0.9 = 6.39
6.8 ×0.5 = 3.40 | 307.2 ×0.3 = 92.16
919.7 ×0.6 = 551.82 | 453.6 ×0.4 = 181.44
54.5 ×0.2 = 10.90 | 79.4 ×0.7 = 55.58

Taking It to the Bank

Name _____ Date _____

Multiply.
Show your work.

$6.15 ×4 = $24.60
$3.53 ×7 = $24.71
$9.81 ×9 = $88.29
$26.32 ×2 = $52.64
$2.19 ×5 = $10.95
$7.34 ×8 = $58.72
$8.62 ×5 = $43.10
$5.76 ×3 = $17.28
$10.81 ×6 = $64.86
$6.89 ×4 = $27.56
$30.25 ×7 = $211.75
$1.73 ×2 = $3.46
$6.24 ×8 = $49.92
$4.31 ×9 = $38.79
$2.27 ×3 = $6.81
$12.62 ×4 = $50.48
$3.87 ×6 = $23.22
$5.22 ×3 = $15.66

Oinkville National Bank — Pennies

The Crooning Crickets

Name _____ Date _____

Read.
Solve each problem on another sheet of paper.
Write the answer in the blank.

The Crooning Crickets—Three Nights Only!

1. Seven friends went to the Crooning Crickets concert. Each ticket cost $9.75. How much did the friends pay for their tickets in all? __$68.25__

2. During the concert, Carl bought 3 sodas. Each soda cost $1.98. How much did he pay in all? __$5.94__

3. T-shirts were on sale for $21.25 each. Carrie bought 2 T-shirts. How much did she pay in all? __$42.50__

4. Carla purchased 4 videos of the band. Each video cost $8.99. How much did she pay in all? __$35.96__

5. Cole bought 6 of the band's CDs for his family. Each CD cost $7.48. How much did he pay in all? __$44.88__

6. Connie bought 5 posters of the band. Each poster cost $2.35. How much did she pay in all? __$11.75__

Push It!

Name _____ Date _____

Multiply.
Show your work.
Write each answer in the magic square. The sum of each row and column should equal 100.

1) 33.92 ×2.54 = 86.1568
2) 4.92 ×0.35 = 1.722
3) 3.64 ×3.33 = 12.1212
4) 1.884 ×0.09 = 0.16956
5) 11.47 ×6.52 = 74.7844
6) 5.25 ×4.48 = 23.5200
7) 303.69 ×0.04 = 12.1476
8) 97.89 ×0.24 = 23.4936
9) 292.54 ×0.22 = 64.3588

1) 86.1568	2) 1.722	3) 12.1212
4) 0.16956	5) 74.7844	6) 23.5200
7) 12.1476	8) 23.4936	9) 64.3588

Just a little more! COACH

Cooling Off

Name _____ Date _____

Multiply.
Show your work on another sheet of paper.
Cross off each answer on the handle.

5.2 × 4 = 20.8
3.9 × 8 = 31.2
1.74 × 6 = 10.44
8.7 × 9 = 78.3
3.04 × 2 = 6.08
2.76 × 5 = 13.8
1.17 × 3 = 3.51
28.8 × 7 = 201.6
1.01 × 5 = 5.05
7.25 × 6 = 43.5
46.3 × 2 = 92.6
2.78 × 4 = 11.12
3.45 × 8 = 27.6
9.21 × 5 = 46.05
6.04 × 3 = 18.12
8.52 × 7 = 59.64
7.03 × 2 = 14.06
16.1 × 7 = 112.7

Handle list:
18.12
11.12
10.44
201.6
59.64
92.6
20.8
6.08
14.06
78.3
13.8
112.7
31.2
43.5
5.05
46.05
27.6

High Dive

Name _____ Date _____

Read.
Show your work on another sheet of paper.
Write the answer in the blank.

All-Ocean High Dive Championship 8.25

1. At the All-Ocean High Dive Championship, 5 divers from the Whales each received a score of 9.13. What was the divers' total score? __45.65__

2. On the Seals team, 6 divers each received a score of 8.75. What was the divers' total score? __52.5__

3. Three divers from the Eels each received a score of 6.3. What was the divers' total score? __18.9__

4. In the final round, 2 divers from the Sea Lions each received a score of 9.97. What was the divers' total score? __19.94__

5. On the Sharks team, 8 divers each received a score of 8.9. What was the divers' total score? __71.2__

6. Four divers from the Otters each received a score of 9.5. What was the divers' total score? __38__

Time for a Mint?

Name _____ Date _____

Multiply.
Show your work on another sheet of paper.
Color if correct.

8.3 × 2.5 = 15.75
17.4 × 5.9 = 102.66
50.1 × 3.8 = 19.039
6.07 × 24.9 = 151.143
1.8 × 4.06 = 7.38
93.25 × 0.5 = 46.525
8.4 × 3.33 = 28.0386
2.47 × 3.04 = 7.588
7.5 × 3.29 = 246.75
4.08 × 0.71 = 2.8968
44.5 × 3.3 = 150.15
61.8 × 5.31 = 328.158
170.3 × 9.2 = 1,566.76
351.2 × 6.89 = 24,197.68
33.62 × 4.68 = 438.1416
104.15 × 35.02 = 3,647.3330
27.43 × 81.6 = 238.288

After Dinner Mints

Sunbather

Name ___ Date ___

Multiply.
Show your work.
Color by the code.

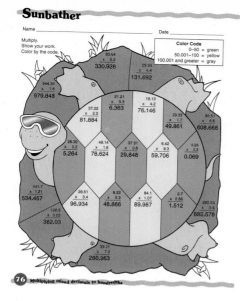

$83.54 \times 5.2 = 330.928$

$29.93 \times 4.4 = 131.692$

$544.36 \times 1.8 = 979.848$

$21.21 \times 0.3 = 6.363$

$18.13 \times 4.2 = 76.146$

$37.22 \times 2.2 = 81.884$

$29.33 \times 1.7 = 49.861$

$90.4 \times 6.6 = 608.668$

$26.32 \times 0.2 = 5.264$

$49.14 \times 1.6 = 78.624$

$37.31 \times 0.8 = 29.848$

$6.42 \times 9.3 = 59.706$

$0.23 \times 0.3 = 0.069$

$447.7 \times 1.21 = 534.457$

$28.51 \times 3.4 = 96.934$

$9.22 \times 5.3 = 48.866$

$84.1 \times 1.07 = 89.987$

$2.7 \times 0.56 = 1.512$

$282.53 \times 2.6 = 682.578$

$128.5 \times 3.02 = 382.03$

$39.31 \times 7.3 = 286.953$

76 — Multiplying mixed decimals to hundredths

Going Home to Roost

Name ___ Date ___

Divide.
Show your work.
Color the shapes with answers less than 20 to show the path home.

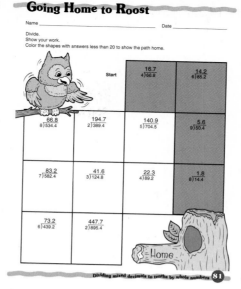

Start	16.7 $4)66.8$	14.2 $6)85.2$
66.8 $8)534.4$	194.7 $2)389.4$	140.9 $5)704.5$	5.6 $9)50.4$
83.2 $7)582.4$	41.6 $3)124.8$	22.3 $4)89.2$	1.8 $8)14.4$
73.2 $6)439.2$	447.7 $2)895.4$		

Home

Dividing mixed decimals to tenths by whole numbers 81

What Has Four Wheels and Flies?

Name ___ Date ___

Divide.
Show your work.
To solve the riddle, match the letters to the numbered lines below.

9.171 (C) $2)18.342$ 162.479 (B) $4)649.916$ 0.414 (A) $6)2.484$ 9.427 (R) $8)75.416$

1.996 (T) $3)5.988$ 12.299 (E) $5)61.495$ 4.863 (R) $7)34.041$ 95.715 (A) $9)861.435$

3.924 (G) $2)7.848$ 2.624 (!) $4)10.496$ 1.274 (G) $6)7.644$ 30.851 (U) $8)246.808$

15.226 (A) $3)45.678$ 197.531 (K) $5)987.655$

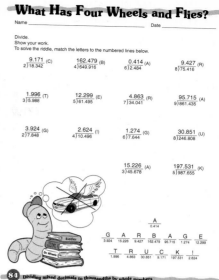

A
0.414

G	A	R	B	A	G	E
3.924	15.226	9.427	162.479	95.715	1.274	12.299

T	R	U	C	K	!
1.996	4.863	30.851	9.171	197.531	2.624

84 — Dividing mixed decimals to thousandths by whole numbers

Getting a Kick Out of Practice

Name ___ Date ___

Multiply.
Show your work on another sheet.
Color the football that contains the answer.

$5.45 \times 16.2 = 88.29$

$0.31 \times 2.8 = 0.868$

$7.24 \times 3.6 = 26.064$

$92.72 \times 4.55 = 421.876$

$4.08 \times 7.2 = 29.376$

$73.57 \times 9.31 = 684.9367$

$8.3 \times 6.57 = 54.531$

$20.49 \times 3.36 = 68.8464$

$11.68 \times 9.8 = 114.464$

$3.25 \times 24.2 = 78.65$

$6.91 \times 8.44 = 58.3204$

$4.12 \times 5.18 = 21.3416$

$61.53 \times 3.9 = 239.967$

$27.5 \times 9.14 = 251.35$

Footballs: 684.9367, 114.464, 0.868, 78.65, 21.3416, 421.876, 54.531, 239.967, 26.064, 29.376, 58.3204, 88.29, 68.8464, 251.35

Multiplying mixed decimals to hundredths 77

Underwater Communication

Name ___ Date ___

Divide.
Show your work.

9.85 $7)68.95$ 3.54 $9)31.86$

18.84 $5)94.20$ 56.47 $3)169.41$

51.73 $4)206.92$ 238.29 $2)476.58$ 11.81 $6)70.86$ 77.67 $7)543.69$

23.75 $9)213.75$ 17.21 $5)86.05$ 31.58 $3)94.74$ 84.68 $4)338.72$

What should fish use to call each other?
To solve the riddle, color the letters of the matching answers.

A W S H E L L O
U P H O N E!

82 — Dividing mixed decimals to hundredths by whole numbers

Having a Ball at the Putting Green!

Name ___ Date ___

Divide.
Show your work.

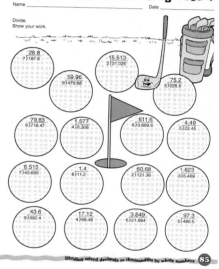

26.8 $7)187.6$

15.513 $2)31.026$

59.96 $8)479.68$ 75.2 $3)225.6$

79.83 $9)718.47$ 1.577 $4)6.308$ 611.6 $6)3,669.6$ 4.49 $5)22.45$

6.515 $7)45.605$ 1.4 $8)11.2$ 60.68 $2)121.36$ 1.823 $3)5.469$

43.6 $9)392.4$ 17.12 $4)68.48$ 3.649 $6)21.894$ 97.3 $5)486.5$

Dividing mixed decimals to thousandths by whole numbers 85

Creepy, Crawly Cup

Name ___ Date ___

Multiply.
Show your work on another sheet of paper.
Color to show the path to the winner.

Cup Finals

$5.073 \times 21.2 =$	107.5476	106.5475	10,754.76	107.95302
$74.415 \times 3.72 =$	2,768.238	276.82380	276.82387	276.82330
$0.862 \times 0.56 =$	0.48272	48.48272	4.82720	0.48278
$29.041 \times 32.78 =$	95.19638	951.96398	951.96399	95.19639
$1.96 \times 0.4 =$	7.84	0.770	0.784	0.780
$83.145 \times 21.33 =$	17.73482	1,774.48280	1,773.48285	1,775.48280
$7.2 \times 1.52 =$	10.914	109.44	11.014	10.944
$68.047 \times 36.84 =$	25,068.514	250.68514	2,506.85148	2,506.85141
$9.431 \times 4.3 =$	40.5534	4,055.33	39.5564	40.5533
$0.936 \times 0.52 =$	4.86722	0.48678	0.48672	1.4560
$0.815 \times 2.33 =$	0.18989	1.89895	2.11450	0.18988
$7.064 \times 64.98 =$	459.01872	71.01962	45,901.872	459.01852
$563.118 \times 0.3 =$	168.6341	168.9354	168.9341	1,689.354
$46.998 \times 3.86 =$	181.41228	138.41224	18,141.2240	50.35804

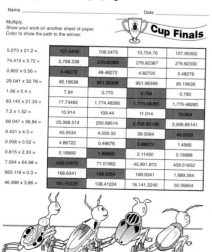

78 — Multiplying mixed decimals to thousandths

Got Grapes?

Name ___ Date ___

Divide.
Show your work on another sheet of paper.
Color by the code.

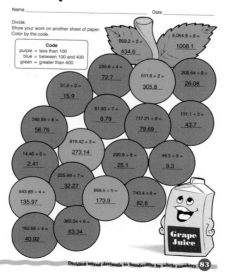

$869.2 \div 2 = 434.6$

$8,064.8 \div 8 = 1008.1$

$290.8 \div 4 = 72.7$

$611.6 \div 2 = 305.8$

$208.64 \div 8 = 26.08$

$31.8 \div 2 = 15.9$

$61.53 \div 7 = 8.79$

$717.21 \div 9 = 79.69$

$131.1 \div 3 = 43.7$

$340.56 \div 6 = 56.76$

$819.42 \div 3 = 273.14$

$200.8 \div 8 = 25.1$

$46.5 \div 5 = 9.3$

$14.46 \div 6 = 2.41$

$225.89 \div 7 = 32.27$

$869.5 \div 5 = 173.9$

$743.4 \div 9 = 82.6$

$543.88 \div 4 = 135.97$

$380.04 \div 6 = 63.34$

$163.68 \div 4 = 40.92$

Grape Juice

Dividing mixed decimals to hundredths by whole numbers 83

Close Companions

Name ___ Date ___

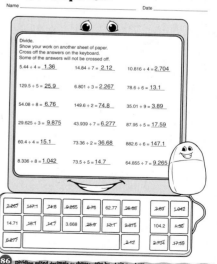

Divide.
Show your work on another sheet of paper.
Cross off the answers on the keyboard.
Some of the answers will not be crossed off.

$5.44 \div 4 = 1.36$ $14.84 \div 7 = 2.12$ $10.816 \div 4 = 2.704$

$129.5 \div 5 = 25.9$ $6.801 \div 3 = 2.267$ $78.6 \div 6 = 13.1$

$54.08 \div 8 = 6.76$ $149.6 \div 2 = 74.8$ $35.01 \div 9 = 3.89$

$29.625 \div 3 = 9.875$ $43.939 \div 7 = 6.277$ $87.95 \div 5 = 17.59$

$60.4 \div 4 = 15.1$ $73.36 \div 2 = 36.68$ $882.6 \div 6 = 147.1$

$8.336 \div 8 = 1.042$ $73.5 \div 5 = 14.7$ $64.855 \div 7 = 9.265$

2.267	147.1	74.8	9.265	8.76	62.77	36.68		3.89	1.042
14.71	38.1	14.7	3.668	25.9	13.1	9.875		104.2	1.36
9.277						2.12	2.704	17.59

86 — Dividing mixed decimals to thousandths by whole numbers

Soup's On!

Name _____ Date _____

Read.
Solve each problem on another sheet of paper.
Write the answer in the blank.

1. Chef Fred sliced 10.8-inch stalks of celery into pieces for his soup. If he cut each stalk into 4 equal pieces, how long was each piece?

    2.7 inches

2. Fred chopped 8.28-inch slices of bacon into pieces. If he cut each slice into 6 equal pieces, how long was each piece?

    1.38 inches

3. Fred's assistant cut 6.335-inch chicken strips into chunks. If he cut each strip into 5 equal chunks, how long was each chunk?

    1.267 inches

4. Fred's assistant also diced 120.6-centimeter strips of potato. If he diced each strip into 9 equal pieces, how long was each piece?

    13.4 centimeters

5. Chef Fred cut 71.52-centimeter strips of green pepper into pieces. If he cut each strip into 8 equal pieces, how long was each piece?

    8.94 centimeters

6. Fred also sliced 273.182-centimeter strips of carrot into pieces. If he cut each strip into 7 equal pieces, how long was each piece?

    39.026 centimeters

Story problems: dividing mixed decimals to thousandths by whole numbers **87**

Shoot for the Stars

Name _____ Date _____

Divide.
Show your work.

$\frac{20}{0.25\,)\,5}$

$\frac{50}{0.36\,)\,18}$

$\frac{400}{0.14\,)\,56}$

$\frac{1300}{0.03\,)\,39}$

$\frac{140}{0.05\,)\,7}$

$\frac{200}{0.33\,)\,66}$

$\frac{8}{0.25\,)\,2}$

$\frac{300}{0.28\,)\,84}$

$\frac{25}{0.64\,)\,16}$

$\frac{400}{0.17\,)\,68}$

$\frac{150}{0.22\,)\,33}$

$\frac{300}{0.27\,)\,81}$

$\frac{50}{0.06\,)\,3}$

$\frac{500}{0.15\,)\,75}$

$\frac{400}{0.24\,)\,96}$

90 Dividing whole numbers by decimals to hundredths

Talk of the Pond

Name _____ Date _____

Divide.
Show your work.

She's here!

$\frac{28}{1.2\,)\,33.6}$

$\frac{2.4}{3.5\,)\,8.4}$

$\frac{14.5}{4.6\,)\,66.7}$

$\frac{19}{8.1\,)\,153.9}$

$\frac{2.5}{2.6\,)\,6.5}$

$\frac{18.04}{62.5\,)\,1,127.5}$

$\frac{0.75}{41.2\,)\,30.9}$

$\frac{7.25}{18.8\,)\,136.3}$

$\frac{82.25}{7.2\,)\,592.2}$

$\frac{15.25}{5.6\,)\,85.4}$

$\frac{76.125}{9.6\,)\,730.8}$

$\frac{97.2}{0.5\,)\,48.6}$

Dividing mixed decimals to tenths **93**

Tools of the Trade

Name _____ Date _____

Read.
Solve each problem on another sheet of paper.
Write the answer in the blank.

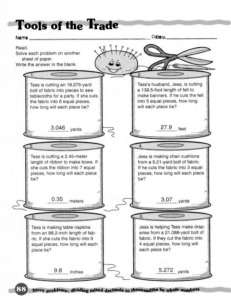

1. Tess is cutting an 18.276-yard bolt of fabric into pieces to sew tablecloths for a party. If she cuts the fabric into 6 equal pieces, how long will each piece be?

    3.046 yards

2. Tess's husband, Jess, is cutting a 139.5-foot length of felt to make banners. If he cuts the felt into 5 equal pieces, how long will each piece be?

    27.9 feet

3. Tess is cutting a 2.45-meter length of ribbon to make bows. If she cuts the ribbon into 7 equal pieces, how long will each piece be?

    0.35 meters

4. Jess is making chair cushions from a 9.21-yard bolt of fabric. If he cuts the fabric into 3 equal pieces, how long will each piece be?

    3.07 yards

5. Tess is making table napkins from an 88.2-inch length of fabric. If she cuts the fabric into 9 equal pieces, how long will each piece be?

    9.8 inches

6. Jess is helping Tess make draperies from a 21.088-yard bolt of fabric. If they cut the fabric into 4 equal pieces, how long will each piece be?

    5.272 yards

88 Story problems: dividing mixed decimals to thousandths by whole numbers

I'll Have the Cheese, Please

Name _____ Date _____

Divide.
Show your work on another sheet of paper.
Color if correct. Connect the colored boxes to draw a path to the finish.

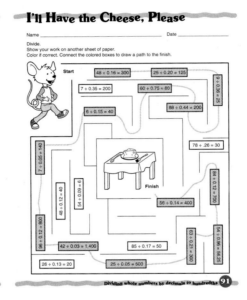

Start

48 ÷ 0.16 = 300   25 ÷ 0.20 = 125

7 ÷ 0.35 = 200   60 ÷ 0.75 = 80

6 ÷ 0.15 = 40   88 ÷ 0.44 = 200

78 ÷ .26 = 30

7 ÷ 0.05 = 140

48 ÷ 0.12 = 40   54 ÷ 0.09 = 6

Finish

56 ÷ 0.14 = 400

96 ÷ 0.12 = 800

42 ÷ 0.03 = 1,400   85 ÷ 0.17 = 50

26 ÷ 0.13 = 20   25 ÷ 0.05 = 500

Dividing whole numbers by decimals to hundredths **91**

A Friendly Rematch

Name _____ Date _____

Divide.
Show your work.
Cross off each matching answer on the grass.
Some answers will not be crossed off.

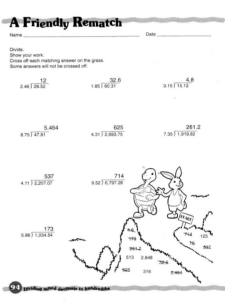

$\frac{12}{2.46\,)\,29.52}$

$\frac{32.6}{1.85\,)\,60.31}$

$\frac{4.8}{3.15\,)\,15.12}$

$\frac{5.464}{8.75\,)\,47.81}$

$\frac{625}{4.31\,)\,2,693.75}$

$\frac{261.2}{7.35\,)\,1,919.82}$

$\frac{537}{4.11\,)\,2,207.07}$

$\frac{714}{9.52\,)\,6,797.28}$

$\frac{173}{5.98\,)\,1,034.54}$

714   125

178   537

261.2

513   2.848   32.6

825   316   5.464

94 Dividing mixed decimals to hundredths

Circus Switcheroo

Name _____ Date _____

Divide.
Show your work.
Write each answer in the magic square.
The sum of each row and column should equal 200.

① $\frac{60}{0.6\,)\,36}$ ② $\frac{70}{0.5\,)\,35}$ ③ $\frac{30}{0.3\,)\,9}$ ④ $\frac{40}{0.5\,)\,20}$

⑤ $\frac{50}{0.2\,)\,10}$ ⑥ $\frac{30}{0.4\,)\,12}$ ⑦ $\frac{45}{0.2\,)\,9}$ ⑧ $\frac{75}{0.8\,)\,60}$

⑨ $\frac{70}{0.7\,)\,49}$ ⑩ $\frac{20}{0.2\,)\,4}$ ⑪ $\frac{35}{0.2\,)\,7}$ ⑫ $\frac{75}{0.4\,)\,30}$

⑬ $\frac{20}{0.9\,)\,18}$ ⑭ $\frac{80}{0.8\,)\,64}$ ⑮ $\frac{90}{0.3\,)\,27}$ ⑯ $\frac{10}{0.6\,)\,6}$

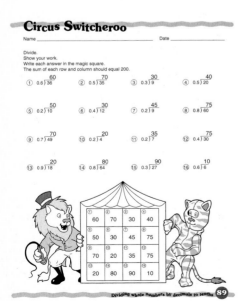

① 60	② 70	③ 30	④ 40
⑤ 50	⑥ 30	⑦ 45	⑧ 75
⑨ 70	⑩ 20	⑪ 35	⑫ 75
⑬ 20	⑭ 80	⑮ 90	⑯ 10

Dividing whole numbers by decimals to tenths **89**

Pinching Pennies

Name _____ Date _____

Read.
Solve each problem on another sheet of paper.
Write the answer in the blank.

1. Pete is saving $0.45 each week to buy a video game that costs $9.00. How many weeks will he have to save?

    20 weeks

2. Each week, Patsy saves $0.75 so she can purchase a shirt that costs $15.00. How many weeks will she have to save?

    20 weeks

3. Pablo is saving $0.12 a day to buy a book. If the book costs $6.00, how many days will he have to save to have enough money to buy the book?

    50 days

4. Each week, Patrick sets aside $0.32 from his allowance. He wants to buy a game that costs $16.00. How many weeks will he have to save?

    50 weeks

5. Paige saves $0.80 each month to buy a CD that costs $12.00. How many months will she have to save in order to buy the CD?

    15 months

6. Each week, Parker saves $0.25 so he can buy a movie that costs $8.00. How many weeks will he have to save?

    32 weeks

7. Paula saves $0.30 a day so she can buy a DVD that costs $18.00. How many days will she need to save in order to have enough to buy the DVD?

    60 days

OINK-MART

92 Story problems: dividing whole numbers by decimals to hundredths

Hot on the Ice-Cream Trail

Name _____ Date _____

Divide.
Show your work on another sheet of paper.
Color if correct to show the path to the ice-cream truck.

Start

$\frac{\$5}{1.25\,)\,\$6.25}$ $\frac{115}{3.41\,)\,392.15}$

$\frac{71.5}{6.32\,)\,451.88}$ $\frac{265}{4.12\,)\,109.18}$ $\frac{\$6.65}{3.33\,)\,\$2,221.11}$ $\frac{3.45}{4.06\,)\,140.07}$

$\frac{31}{7.14\,)\,221.34}$ $\frac{\$265}{2.47\,)\,\$654.55}$ $\frac{.277}{1.58\,)\,43.45}$ $\frac{23.5}{5.43\,)\,124.89}$

$\frac{\$.053}{8.25\,)\,\$437.25}$ $\frac{161}{5.61\,)\,903.21}$ $\frac{1.27}{2.56\,)\,440.32}$ $\frac{403.3}{3.71\,)\,1,495.13}$

Finish

$\frac{44.3}{6.65\,)\,288.61}$ $\frac{\$65}{2.55\,)\,\$165.75}$ $\frac{\$25}{4.95\,)\,\$123.75}$

Dividing mixed decimals to hundredths **95**

Spelling Surprise

Name _____ Date _____

Divide.
Show your work on another sheet of paper.
Write the answer on the blank.
To solve the riddle, color the letters that have matching answers.

What word is always spelled incorrectly?

396.36 ÷ 1.08 = __367__

50.88 ÷ 4.24 = __12__   982.52 ÷ 8.47 = __116__

31.28 ÷ 7.36 = __4.25__   1,443.18 ÷ 3.59 = __402__

52.44 ÷ 9.12 = __5.75__   627.12 ÷ 2.01 = __312__

239.61 ÷ 1.63 = __147__   146.28 ÷ 5.52 = __26.5__

193.41 ÷ 3.15 = __61.4__   232.22 ÷ 6.83 = __34__

96 Dividing mixed decimals to hundredths

Page 103
Checkup 1
Test A
A. eight and twenty-four hundredths, seventeen and eight tenths
B. thirty-five and four hundred twelve thousandths, two hundred five and thirty-seven hundredths.
C. 7.9
D. 15.35
E. 63.062
F. 304.91
G. 84.07
H. 502.101

Test B
A. six and thirty-five hundredths, twenty-two and four tenths
B. fifty-one and seventy-seven hundredths, one hundred eight and six hundred twenty-seven thousandths
C. 5.6
D. 27.13
E. 82.035
F. 493.42
G. 90.002
H. 305.7

Page 105
Checkup 2
Test A
A. <, >
B. <, <
C. >, <
D. 0.83, 0.89, 0.9; 2.5, 2.52, 2.57
E. 8.04, 8.14, 8.4; 3.61, 3.63, 3.68

Test B
A. <, <
B. >, >
C. >, <
D. 4.01, 4.1, 4.17; 2.05, 2.51, 2.55
E. 6.35, 6.5, 6.53; 0.8, 0.81, 0.82

Page 107
Checkup 3
Test A
A. 55.5, $27.01, 11.75, 34.53
B. 26.9, $49.92
C. 57.035, 24.48
D. 285.97, $78.17

Test B
A. 7.5, $12.83, 54.11, 23.855
B. 102.5, $34.91
C. 26.175, 48.94
D. 1,102.813, $32.57

Page 109
Checkup 4
Test A
A. 10.25, 13.05, 11.22, 32.48
B. 52.25, 10.29
C. 59.25, 78.44
D. 41.99, 172.95

Test B
A. 9.15, 24.39, 20.56, 43.77
B. 54.98, 16.23
C. 31.04, 18.22
D. 61.46, 231.98

Page 111
Checkup 5
Test A
A. 10.58, 17.384, 29.665, 603.09
B. 45.452, 10.468
C. 125.575, 13.384
D. 57.87, 396.434

Test B
A. 21.796, 13.15, 43.628, 287.4
B. 32.906, 7.528
C. 259.145, 16.502
D. 58.92, 221.819

Page 113
Checkup 6
Test A
A. 38.2, $67.25, 238.7, 15.125
B. 16.5, $460.78
C. 72.28, 61.5
D. 2.225, 14.136

Test B
A. 8.7, $4.69, 57.13, 13.115
B. $21.85, 53.072
C. 422.8, 70.55
D. 9.238, 202.4

Page 115
Checkup 7
Test A
A. 3.46, 5.44, 8.18, 22.75
B. 1.63, 1.75
C. 36.05, 30.35
D. 80.58, 25.69

Test B
A. 2.48, 2.83, 7.73, 4.32
B. 7.51, 7.11
C. 13.68, 41.26
D. 25.45, 74.75

Page 117
Checkup 8
Test A
A. 12.248, 8.116, 2.211, 18.552
B. 14.222, 6.656
C. 12.468, 49.412
D. 33.281, 81.615

Test B
A. 6.877, 6.739, 4.647, 21.284
B. 23.101, 4.944
C. 27.454, 69.384
D. 30.832, 55.107

Page 119
Checkup 9
Test A
A. 1.23, 1.68, 5.46, 28.8
B. 11.4, 0.75, 64.4, 24.82
C. 7.2, 10.8
D. 2.35, 16.2

Test B
A. 3.0, 3.51, 8.91, 46.8
B. 10.08, 56.8, 0.85, 9.45
C. 4.14, 27.5
D. 67.6, 4.42

Page 121
Checkup 10
Test A
A. 0.12, 0.30, 0.135, 0.328
B. 0.1764, 0.0384, 0.273, 0.2475
C. 0.28, 0.27
D. 0.384, 0.2842

Test B
A. 0.42, 0.36, 0.068, 0.434
B. 0.1196, 0.1026, 0.156, 0.1444
C. 0.40, 0.16
D. 0.222, 0.2465

Page 123
Checkup 11
Test A
A. 20, 31.5, 19.32, 15.18
B. 82.6, 14.34, 46, 32.8
C. 22.2, 96.8
D. 51.2, 36.24

Test B
A. 115.2, 25.48, 12, 34.4
B. 29.16, 14.82, 42.4, 71.4
C. 54.4, 22.89
D. 32.52, 84.6

Page 125
Checkup 12
Test A
A. 14.84, 15.19, 4.301, 23.744
B. 30.125, 15.5482, 8.5767
C. 138.24, 31.04, 14.9144

Test B
A. 14.95, 32.4, 24.395, 59.5
B. 28.8648, 9.5853, 6.86036
C. 9.12, 56.85867, 28.7543

Page 127
Checkup 13
Test A
A. 1.14, 0.43, 3.1, 1.37
B. 6.8, 0.346, 0.971, 5.3
C. 1.379, 1.37
D. 6.092, 3.198

Test B
A. 0.69, 0.35, 7.2, 2.4
B. 0.799, 0.27, 0.33, 7.1
C. 3.198, 0.212
D. 6.6, 6.14

Page 129
Checkup 14
Test A
A. 200, $300, 30
B. 20, 200, 20
C. 50, 20, $50
D. 900, $200, 200

Test B
A. 30, 40, 40
B. $500, 200, 50
C. 30, 200, $50
D. 130, 200, 400

Page 131
Checkup 15
Test A
A. 3.5, 6, 1.2
B. 6.2, 43
C. 8.5, 9.5

Test B
A. 5, 9.5, 12
B. 22, 6.5
C. 3.25, 8.4

Decimals

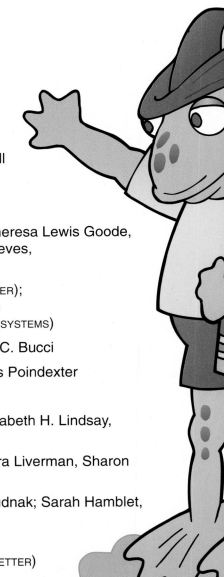

Managing Editor: Debra Liverman

Editor at Large: Diane Badden

Staff Editors: Lauren E. Cox, Peggy W. Hambright, Sherry McGregor, Cindy Mondello

Copy Editors: Tazmen Carlisle, Amy Kirtley-Hill, Kristy Parton, Debbie Shoffner, Cathy Edwards Simrell

Cover Artist: Kimberly Richard

Art Coordinator: Pam Crane

Artists: Pam Crane, Chris Curry, Shane Freeman, Theresa Lewis Goode, Clevell Harris, Ivy L. Koonce, Clint Moore, Greg D. Rieves, Rebecca Saunders, Barry Slate, Donna K. Teal

The Mailbox® Books.com: Judy P. Wyndham (MANAGER); Jennifer Tipton Bennett (DESIGNER/ARTIST); Karen White (INTERNET COORDINATOR); Paul Fleetwood, Xiaoyun Wu (SYSTEMS)

President, The Mailbox Book Company™: Joseph C. Bucci

Director of Book Planning and Development: Chris Poindexter

Curriculum Director: Karen P. Shelton

Book Development Managers: Cayce Guiliano, Elizabeth H. Lindsay, Thad McLaurin

Editorial Planning: Kimberley Bruck (DIRECTOR); Debra Liverman, Sharon Murphy, Susan Walker (TEAM LEADERS)

Editorial and Freelance Management: Karen A. Brudnak; Sarah Hamblet, Hope Rodgers (EDITORIAL ASSISTANTS)

Editorial Production: Lisa K. Pitts (TRAFFIC MANAGER); Lynette Dickerson (TYPE SYSTEMS); Mark Rainey (TYPESETTER)

Librarian: Dorothy C. McKinney

www.themailbox.com